HARCOURT SCIENCE

WORKBOOK

Harcourt School Publishers

Orlando • Boston • Dallas • Chicago • San Diego

www.harcourtschool.com

Harcourt

Contents

Harcourt

Harcourt

Safety in Science

Here are some safety rules to follow.

1 Think ahead. Study the steps and safety symbols of the investigation so you know what to expect. If you have any questions, ask your teacher.

2 Be neat. Keep your work area clean. If you have long hair, pull it back so it doesn't get in the way. Roll up long sleeves. If you should spill or break something, or get cut, tell your teacher right away.

3 Watch your eyes. Wear safety goggles when told to do so.

4 Yuck! Never eat or drink anything during a science activity unless you are told to do so by your teacher.

5 Don't get shocked. Be sure that electric cords are in a safe place where you can't trip over them. Don't ever pull a plug out of an outlet by pulling on the cord.

6 Keep it clean. Always clean up when you have finished. Put everything away and wash your hands.

In some activities you will see these symbols. They are signs for what you need to do to be safe.

CAUTION
Be especially careful.

CAUTION
Wear safety goggles.

CAUTION
Be careful with sharp objects.

CAUTION
Don't get burned.

CAUTION
Protect your clothes.

CAUTION
Protect your hands with mitts.

CAUTION
Be careful with electricity.

Harcourt

Science Safety

_____ I will study the steps of the investigation before I begin.

_____ I will ask my teacher if I do not understand something.

_____ I will keep my work area clean.

_____ I will pull my hair back and roll up long sleeves before I begin.

_____ I will tell my teacher if I spill or break something or get cut.

_____ I will wear safety goggles when I am told to do so.

_____ I will tell my teacher if I get something in my eye.

_____ I will not eat or drink anything during an investigation unless told to do so by my teacher.

_____ I will be extra careful when using electrical appliances.

_____ I will keep electric cords out of the way and only unplug them by pulling on the protected plug.

_____ I will clean up when I am finished.

_____ I will return unused materials to my teacher.

_____ I will wipe my area and then wash my hands.

Harcourt

Chapter 1 • Graphic Organizer for Chapter Concepts

How Plants Grow

LESSON 1
PLANTS

Plants are made of 5. _____

LESSON 2
SIMPLE PLANTS

A simple plant has no

1. _____

2. _____

3. _____

LESSON 3
PLANTS AND SEEDS

Needs of Seeds

1. _____

2. _____

Plants Grow From

1. _____

2. _____

3. _____

Parts of a Seed

1. _____

2. _____

3. _____

How Seeds Are Spread

1. _____

2. _____

3. _____

LESSON 4
FOOD FOR PLANTS

What Plants Need to Make Food

1. _____

2. _____

3. _____

4. _____

How Plants Use Food

1. _____

2. _____

Needs of Plants

Materials

6 young plants   6 paper cups   potting soil   marker

brown paper bag   water   ruler

Activity Procedure

1 Put the plants in the paper cups and add soil. Make sure all six plants have the same amount of soil. Label two of the plants *No Water*. Put these plants in a sunny window.

2 Label two plants *No Light*. Place these plants on a table away from a window. Water the plants. Then cover them with a paper bag.

3 Label the last two plants *Water and Light*. Water these plants. Put them in a sunny window.

4 Every other day for two weeks, **observe** the plants. Check to make sure the plants labeled *No Light* and *Water and Light* have moist soil. Add enough water to keep the soil moist.

5 Record your observations on the chart on the next page. On the chart, **record** any changes you **observe** in the plants. Look for changes in the color and height of each plant.

Harcourt

Name _____

Plants	Day 1	Day 3	Day 5	Day 7	Day 9	Day 11
No Water						
No Light						
Water and Light						

Draw Conclusions

1. Which plants looked the healthiest after two weeks? _____

_____

Why do you think so? _____

_____

2. Which plants looked the least healthy after two weeks?

_____

_____

What was different for these plants? _____

_____

3. Scientists at Work Scientists often **compare** observations to reach their conclusions. Compare your observations of the plants to tell what things plants need to grow. Make a list. _____

_____

_____

_____

Name _____

Date _____

Compare

When you compare, you identify how things are alike and how they are different. You can use your sense of sight when you compare. Comparing helps you gather information.

Think About Comparing

Suppose you plant two tomato plants in rich, dark soil in the back yard. You plant *Plant A* in a place where it gets full sun. You plant *Plant B* in a shady area. You give both plants the same amount of water. At the end of the growing season, *Plant A* is covered with juicy red tomatoes. *Plant B* has only a few tomatoes on it.

Plant A   **Plant B**

1. Compare the size of the two plants. _____

_____

2. Compare the leaf color of the two plants. _____

_____

_____

3. How are the plants different from each other? _____

_____

4. Which growing conditions were the same for both plants?

_____

5. Which growing condition was different? _____

_____

Harcourt

Name _____

Date _____

Use Context to Determine/Confirm Word Meaning

Read the paragraph below. Use your own words to write definitions for the underlined terms. Then use a dictionary to look up the terms. Compare your definitions with the dictionary definitions.

Healthful Foods

    The leaves of many plants can be eaten as food. Many people enjoy eating lettuce, cabbage, or kale. Often, these leafy foods are eaten in salads along with other vegetables. Leafy vegetables are healthful and are good sources of <u>fiber</u>. Fiber cannot be <u>digested</u>, or broken down, but it helps food move through the <u>intestines</u>. Other plant foods that have fiber include Brussels sprouts, lentils, and avocados.

Your Own Words	Dictionary Definition
fiber	**fiber**
digested	**digested**
intestines	**intestines**

Harcourt

Name _____

Date _____

What Is a Plant?

Lesson Concept

Plants have a variety of needs that must be met in order
for them to live and grow.

Vocabulary

root (A7)   **stem** (A7)   **leaf** (A7)   **cell** (A8)

Underline the best answer.

1. Plants get what they need from the sun, air, rain, and ____.

    A plant food   **B** soil   **C** rocks   **D** animals

2. The stem of a plant supports the plant ____.

    A above ground   **C** underground

    B before it sprouts   **D** after it dies

3. Leaves help plants use ____.

    A light and air   **B** fruit   **C** soil   **D** food

**Write the name of the circled part of the plant under each
picture. Use the vocabulary list.**

4.   **5.**   **6.**

_____   _____   _____

Harcourt

Name _____

Date _____

The Parts of a Simple Plant

Materials

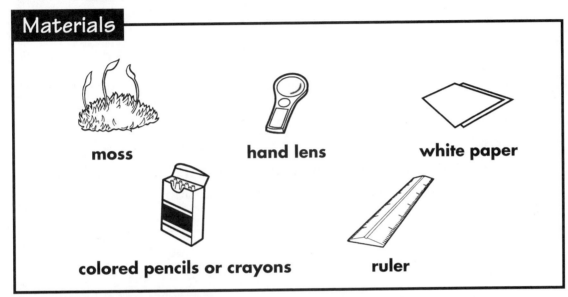

moss   hand lens   white paper

colored pencils or crayons   ruler

Activity Procedure

1 Feel a clump of moss. Describe how it feels. **Observe** it closely with a hand lens. Notice that it is made up of many tiny moss plants growing very close together. (Picture A)

2 Separate a single moss plant from the clump. Place it on a sheet of white paper. (Picture B)

3 **Observe** the stalk with the hand lens. Use colored pencils or crayons to make a drawing of the stalk. Label your drawing *stemlike part*.

4 **Observe** the tiny hairs growing from the bottom of the stemlike part. Add these to your drawing. Label them *rootlike parts*.

5 **Observe** the tiny green, leaflike parts growing around the stem. Feel their texture and thickness. Observe how they are arranged. Add these parts to your drawing. Label them *leaflike parts*.

6 Use the ruler to **measure** the height of the moss plant in millimeters. **Record** this height on your drawing.

Harcourt

Draw Conclusions

1. How is the moss plant like most plants you have seen?

_____

_____

2. How is a moss plant different from most plants you have seen?

_____

_____

3. Scientists at Work Scientists use tools such as microscopes and hand lenses to **observe** living things more closely. What could you see with a hand lens that you could not see with your eyes alone?

_____

_____

_____

_____

Investigate Further Peat moss comes from a type of moss that grows in swamps. Get a cup of dry peat moss and a cup of potting soil. **Record** the mass of each. **Form a hypothesis** about how much water each material can soak up. **Design and conduct an experiment** to test your hypothesis. **Infer** why peat moss is often added to garden soil.

_____

_____

_____

_____

_____

Harcourt

Name _____

Date _____

Observe

When you observe, you use your senses. Sometimes you use all of your senses. At other times you may use only one or two of your senses. Using your senses can help you learn about something.

Think About Observing

Joanne takes a walk through a flower garden. She notices that there are many different types of flowers. They are different shapes, colors, and sizes. Some are big and bushy, while others grow tall. Some are small and grow low to the ground. Joanne observes many different colors. She smells some of the flowers. She feels a few of them. Some are fuzzy or smooth, others are prickly or rough. Joanne observes that each flower is different.

1. When you look at a flower garden, what can you observe?

_____

_____

2. What sense did you use in making this observation?

_____

3. What other senses can you use to tell the different flowers apart?

_____

4. Blooming flowers sometimes attract bees. How can your sense of hearing help you make this observation?

_____

_____

5. Rose stems have thorns. What sense might this affect, and how?

_____

Harcourt

Name _____

Date _____

Identifying Supporting Facts and Details

Read the following paragraph. When you are finished, fill in the graphic organizer below, showing the main idea and supporting facts and details.

Where Simple Plants Grow Best

Because they have no roots, stems, or leaves, simple plants grow best in damp, shady places. Roots, stems and leaves have tubes that carry water to different parts of the plant. Simple plants do not have such tubes. They grow best where they can take their food, water, and nutrients directly from the environment. Without tubes to carry water long distances, they grow small and close to the ground.

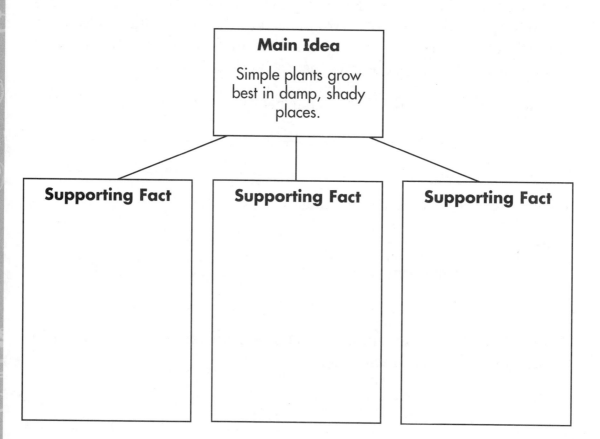

Main Idea

Simple plants grow best in damp, shady places.

Supporting Fact

Supporting Fact

Supporting Fact

Harcourt

Use with page A14.

Name _____

Date _____

What Parts Does a Simple Plant Have?

Lesson Concept

Simple plants have a different form than other plants, such as trees and flowers, do.

Vocabulary

simple plants (A14)	**leaves** (A14)	**roots** (A14)
environment (A14)	**mosses** (A14)	**tubes** (A14)
liverworts (A14)	**stems** (A14)	

Fill in the blanks below, using vocabulary terms from above.

_____ do not grow very big. Simple plants have

no _____, _____, or

_____. Unlike trees and flowers, simple plants do not

have _____ to move water and nutrients to every part.

A simple plant takes in nutrients from its _____.

_____ and _____ are

simple plants.

Harcourt

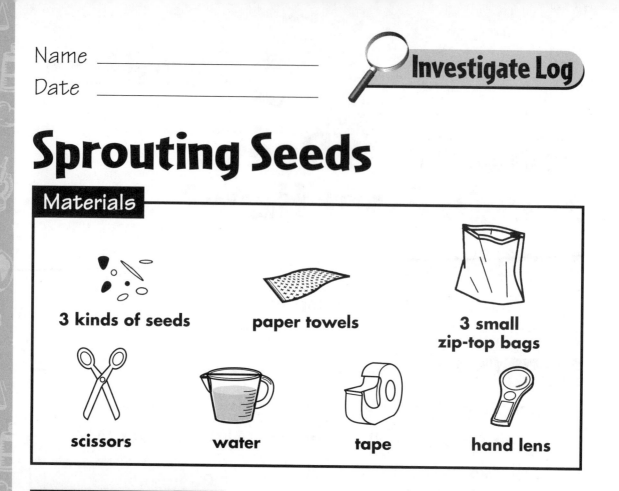

Sprouting Seeds

Materials

- 3 kinds of seeds
- paper towels
- 3 small zip-top bags
- scissors
- water
- tape
- hand lens

Activity Procedure

1 Start with a small amount of mixed seeds. Use size and shape to sort the seeds into three groups.

2 Cut two paper towels in half. Fold the towels to fit into the plastic bags. Add water to make the towels damp. Do not use too much water or you will drown the seeds.

3 Put one group of seeds into each bag, and seal the bags. Label the bags *1, 2,* and *3*. Tape the bags to the inside of a window.

4 Use a hand lens to **observe** the seeds every school day for 10 days. Use the chart below and on the next page to **record** your observations.

Seeds	Days				
	1	2	3	4	5
Group 1					
Group 2					
Group 3					

Harcourt

Name _____

Seeds	Days				
	6	7	8	9	10
Group 1					
Group 2					
Group 3					

Draw Conclusions

1. What changes did you **observe** in the seeds? _____

_____

2. How quickly did the changes take place in the different kinds of seeds?

_____

3. Scientists at Work Scientists **observe** their investigations closely to get new information. How did observing the seeds help you understand

more about seeds? _____

Investigate Further Repeat the investigation steps, but place the bags in a dark closet instead of in a window. **Predict** what will happen. **Record** your observations.

My prediction: _____

_____

_____

My observations: _____

_____

_____

_____

Harcourt

Name _____

Date _____

Observe

You can observe directly with your senses. Or you can use a hand lens or microscope to observe. Making an observation is one of the most basic science skills.

Think About Observing

You are planning a vegetable garden. You order watermelon, corn, butter bean, and cucumber seeds. When the seeds arrive, they are all mixed together in one container! The company has sent colored pictures of the seeds and the vegetables that will grow from the seeds. You can use your observation skills to identify the seeds.

1. You spread the seeds out on a table. Which sense will you use to observe the seeds? _____

2. In what ways are the seeds different from one another?

_____

_____

3. How could a hand lens help you with your observations?

_____

4. Describe what you will do to match the seeds to the seeds in the picture.

Step 1: _____

Step 2: _____

Step 3: _____

5. How did observing help you understand which seeds were which?

_____

_____

Harcourt

Use with page A17.

Name _____

Date _____

Use Graphic Sources for Information

Seeds

Label the parts of the seed. Use the descriptions below.

Seedling: A seedling lives inside every seed.

Seed coat: The seed coat protects the young plant inside the seed.

Stored food: Most of the inside of a seed is stored food. The young plant uses the food to grow when the seed sprouts.

These plants form seeds. Color in and label each seed.

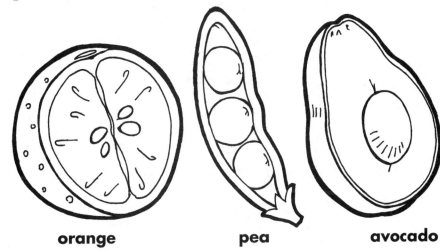

| orange | pea | avocado |

Harcourt

What Kinds of Plants Have Seeds?

Lesson Concept

Seeds produce seedlings that grow into new plants.

Vocabulary

seeds (A18)   **germinate** (A21)   **seedlings** (A21)

Fill in the blank with the correct vocabulary term from the list above.

Some plants form _____ to make new plants.

The small new plants are called _____. Some plants
also can be grown from plant parts. Seeds grow to look like the adult
plants they came from. All seeds have the same parts. Seeds necd water

to _____. Seeds are spread to new places by air,
water, and animals.

For each picture below circle the plant part that makes seeds.

These sentences are mixed up. Number them in order.

_____ The sprout breaks through the soil.

_____ Leaves begin to grow.

_____ A root grows from the seed.

Harcourt

Use with page A25.

Food Factories

Materials

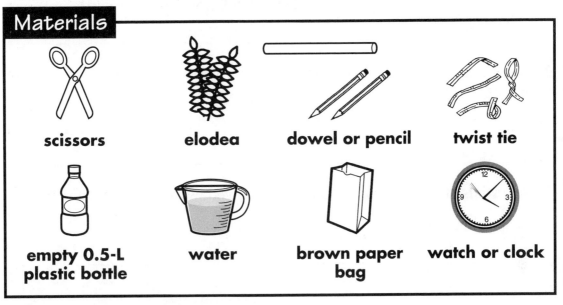

scissors | elodea | dowel or pencil | twist tie

empty 0.5-L plastic bottle | water | brown paper bag | watch or clock

Activity Procedure

1 **CAUTION** **Be careful when using scissors.** Use scissors to cut a piece of elodea (el•oh•DEE•uh) as long as the bottle.

2 Wrap the elodea around the dowel. Use a twist tie to attach it to the dowel.

3 Put the elodea into the bottle, and fill the bottle with water.

4 Put the bottle in a place away from any windows. Cover the bottle with the brown paper bag. After 10 minutes, remove the bag. **Record** any changes you **observe.**

My observations: _____

_____

5 This time, place the bottle in bright sunlight and don't cover it with the brown paper bag. After 10 minutes, **observe** the bottle. **Record** any changes you observe.

My observations: _____

_____

Harcourt

Draw Conclusions

1. Did the elodea and water in the bottle look different after Steps 4 and 5?

_____ If they did, tell how they were different.

_____

2. What did you change between Steps 4 and 5? What remained the same in steps 4 and 5?

_____

_____

3. Scientists at Work From what you **observed**, what can you **infer** about

the bubbles you saw? _____

_____

_____

Investigate Further Scientists often **measure** what happens in experiments. One way to measure what is happening in this experiment is to count the number of bubbles that appear. Put the bottle with the elodea in bright sunlight, and count the number of bubbles that appear in one minute.

My observations: _____

_____

Then move the bottle out of the direct sun. Again count the number of bubbles that appear in one minute.

My observations: _____

_____

How are the two measurements different? **Infer** why they are different.

_____

_____

Harcourt

Name _____

Date _____

Infer

When you infer, you use what you have observed to form an opinion or give an explanation. That opinion is called an inference.

Think About Inferring

You and your friend are having a contest to see who can grow the tallest sunflower. You each plant a seed in your backyard. The seeds germinate and begin to grow. You both give your plants water and fertilizer. The two plants grow taller every day. One day you go out to check your sunflower. You observe that the petals of your sunflower have holes in them. You use your hand lens to examine the whole plant from the flower to where the stem goes into the ground. You see a worm crawling on the flower.

1. What are you trying to explain? _____

   _____

2. What are your observations? _____

   _____

3. What information did you gather? _____

   _____

4. What could you infer about the holes in the petal of the sunflower?

   How would you explain them? _____

   _____

5. Think about your inference. Do you think your plant will grow or die?

   Explain your opinion. _____

   _____

   _____

   _____

Harcourt

Name _____

Date _____

Arrange Events in Sequence

Look at the sentences below. Reorder the sentences and write a paragraph using the sentences.

The plant uses some of the food to grow bigger and make seeds.

People and animals use some of these plant parts as food.

The plant makes sugar and gives off oxygen.

Some plants store some of this food in their roots, stems, and fruits.

A plant takes in sunlight, water, and carbon dioxide.

The chlorophyll in the leaves lets the plant use these things to make food.

_____

_____

_____

_____

_____

_____

_____

Use with page A30.

How Do Plants Make Food?

Lesson Concept

Plants make their own food through the process of
photosynthesis.

Vocabulary

photosynthesis (A28)   **chlorophyll** (A28)

For each pair of sentences, circle the letter of the correct statement.

1. A The substance in plants that makes them green is called
photosynthesis.

  B The substance in plants that makes them green is called chlorophyll.

2. A Photosynthesis is the process plants use to make carbon dioxide.

  B Photosynthesis is the process plants use to make food.

3. A Plants use the food they make to grow bigger and make seeds.

  B Plants use the food they make to produce carbon dioxide.

Circle the parts of each plant where food that humans eat is stored.

Harcourt

Recognize Vocabulary

root	cell	seed	leaves	stem
germinate	chlorophyll	photosynthesis	seedling	

Use the words above to fill in the blanks in the paragraph.

    Two classmates decided to grow two plants for the science fair. First, they filled two clear plastic pots with good soil. They planted one

_____ in each pot. They placed one pot in a sunny window and the other in a closet. They observed their plants each day.

    The seeds began to _____. One day the classmates

saw a _____ growing down into the dirt of each

pot. Next, a young plant called a _____ appeared.

Each plant was supported by a _____.

    The classmates observed that the plant in the closet was no longer

doing well. Its _____ were not green. The

_____ in the plant needed sun to help the plant

make food. The process of _____ could not continue

in the _____ without light.

Draw the stages of the growth of plants. Label each picture. On the last picture, label as many plant parts as you can.

Harcourt

Name _____

Date _____

Compare and Contrast Plants

Informative Writing–Compare and Contrast

Observe two different plants that grow from seeds. Then write a paragraph comparing and contrasting the two plants. Use the chart below to help you list ways the two plants are alike and ways they are different.

Plant 1	Plant 1 and Plant 2	Plant 2
Different	Alike	Different

Harcourt

Use with pages A10–A17.

Chapter 2 • Graphic Organizer for Chapter Concepts

Types of Animals

LESSON 1

Animal Needs

1. _____
2. _____
3. _____
4. _____

LESSON 2

	covered with	breathe with	how born
Mammals	1. _____	2. _____	3. _____
Birds	4. _____	5. _____	6. _____

LESSON 3

	covered with	breathe with	how born
Amphibians	1. _____	2. _____	3. _____
Fish	4. _____	5. _____	6. _____
Reptiles	7. _____	8. _____	9. _____

LESSON 4

Animal Behaviors Are

1. _____
2. _____

To Escape the Cold, Animals

3. _____
4. _____

Animals Are Protected By

5. _____
6. _____

LESSON 5

Extinction: Species can be

1. _____
2. _____
3. _____

Harcourt

Animal Homes

Materials

Animal Picture Cards

Activity Procedure

1 Select six Animal Picture Cards, or use the pictures on page A40. As you **observe** the cards, pay close attention to the types of homes the animals live in.

2 Describe each animal home you **observe**. **Record** your descriptions.

Animal Home 1: _____

_____

Animal Home 2: _____

_____

Animal Home 3: _____

_____

Animal Home 4: _____

_____

Animal Home 5: _____

_____

Animal Home 6: _____

_____

3 With a partner, discuss the different types of animal homes shown. Talk about the ways the animal homes are alike and the ways they are different. Then **classify** the animals by the types of homes they live in.

Harcourt

Name _____

My Classification	
Description	**Animals in the Group**

Draw Conclusions

1. Compare two of the animal homes you observed. Tell how each home helps protect the animal that lives there. _____

_____

_____

2. What did you **observe** about the home of a Canada goose and the home of an albatross? _____

_____

3. Scientists at Work Scientists **classify** animals into groups based on what the animals have in common. How many groups did you classify the animals into? What were the groups? _____

_____

_____

_____

_____

Investigate Further Study the Animal Picture Cards again. This time, look at the body covering of each animal. Describe each covering. How can you use body coverings to **classify** animals? _____

_____

_____

Harcourt

Name _____

Date _____

Classify

Classifying is putting objects into groups according to how they are alike.

Think About Classifying

Your teacher gives you a worksheet showing different animals. You must classify the animals. You decide to classify them based on how they move. In the chart below, list the animals based on how they move.

lion   parrot   sea horse   butterfly   deer

eagle   lizard   whale   shark   owl

dolphin   blue jay   cat   horse   salmon

Classifying Animals by How They Move		
Walking Animals	**Flying Animals**	**Swimming Animals**
lizard		

Harcourt

Name _____

Date _____

Compare and Contrast

Animals need air, water, food, and shelter. Different animals meet their needs in different ways. Use the information below to answer the questions.

Brown Bear • eats plants such as grasses or berries • catches and eats fish	**Robin** • builds nest of leaves, moss, and feathers • uses lungs to breathe
Panda • lives in a mountain forest • eats bamboo plants	**Turtle** • uses its hard shell as its home • eats insects, worms, berries, and mushrooms
Beaver • builds its dam in a stream • uses cut trees, rocks, and mud for dam • uses lungs to breathe	**Whale** • lives in water • uses lungs to breathe

1. Which three animals named above eat plants?

_____

2. How is the home of a turtle different from the home of a robin?

_____

3. How might a robin and a beaver be similar in the way they build their homes?

_____

4. Do pandas and brown bears eat the same kinds of food? Explain.

_____

5. How are a whale and a bird similar?

_____

Harcourt

Name _____

Date _____

Concept Review

What Is an Animal?

Harcourt

Lesson Concept

All animals have needs that must be met in order for them to live.

Vocabulary

traits (A48)	**inherit** (A48)

Fill in each blank with a vocabulary term.

All animals need food, water, air, and shelter. Different animals have different shapes and sizes. They have many different body parts. These shapes, sizes, and different body parts help animals get the things they need.

All animals _____ their features from their parents.

These features are called _____ .

Underline the best answer.

1. The four things that all animals need are ____.
   A food, water, shelter, and air   **C** food, water, heat, and air
   B food, water, sunlight, and air   **D** soil, water, food, and sunlight

2. Animals that live on land get oxygen from ____.
   A the air   **B** food   **C** water   **D** sunlight

3. An animal's body produces energy from ____.
   A coal   **B** food   **C** air   **D** sunlight

4. The bodies of all animals contain ____.
   A water   **B** feathers   **C** fur   **D** scales

5. Caves, nests, turtle shells, and tunnels are all examples of ____.
   A animal shelters   **C** inherited traits
   B food containers   **D** water sources

Fur Helps Animals

Materials

glue

2 metal cans

cotton batting

hot water

2 thermometers

classroom clock

CAUTION Activity Procedure

1. Record your observations on the chart on the next page.

2. Spread glue around the outside of one can. Then put a thick layer of cotton around the can. Wait for the glue to dry. Then use your fingers to fluff the cotton.

3. **CAUTION** **Be careful with the hot water, it can burn you.** Your teacher will fill both cans with hot water.

4. Place a thermometer in each can, and **record** the temperature of the water.

5. Check the temperature of the water in each can every 10 minutes for a period of 30 minutes. **Record** the temperatures on the chart.

Harcourt

Name _____

Time	Water Temperature in Can with Cotton	Water Temperature in Can Without Cotton
Start		
10 min		
20 min		
30 min		

Draw Conclusions

1. In which can did the water stay hot longer? Why? _____

_____

2. How is having fur like wearing a jacket? _____

_____

_____

3. Scientists at Work Scientists often **use a model** to study things they can't observe easily. In this investigation, you made a model of an animal with fur. Why was using a model easier than observing an animal?

_____

_____

Investigate Further How do you think your results would be different if you used ice-cold water instead of hot water? Write a **hypothesis** and conduct an experiment to find out.

My hypothesis: _____

_____

_____

Harcourt

Name _____

Date _____

Use a Model

Using a model can help you study things you cannot observe easily.

Think About Using a Model

A polar bear has black skin. The polar bear's skin takes in the heat from the sun. You decide to make a model to test this idea. On a warm, sunny day, you take four ice cubes out of the freezer. You wrap two ice cubes in black plastic and two in white plastic. You put the two packets on a tray and set it outside in the sun. You want to find out which packet of ice cubes absorbs the heat more quickly. You time which packet of ice cubes melts faster. You feel each packet at five-minute intervals. You find out that the ice in the black plastic melted faster than the ice in the white plastic.

1. Why would you use a model to find out about the heat absorption of the polar bear's skin? _____

   _____

2. What observations can you make? _____

   _____

   _____

3. What comparisons can you make between the two packets?

   _____

   _____

4. Use your observations to infer why the ice in the black packet melted

   faster than the ice in the white packet. _____

   _____

   _____

5. What might this model tell you about the polar bear's skin?

   _____

   _____

Harcourt

Use with page A51.

Name _____

Date _____

Summarize and Paraphrase a Selection

Bird Beaks and Feet

You can learn a lot about a bird by looking at its beak and its feet. The shape of a bird's beak can tell you what that bird eats. For example, a pelican is a water bird with a pouch that extends from its throat. The pelican uses its beak and throat pouch to scoop up fish, much like we use a net to catch fish. Many vultures have strong, heavy beaks, which they use for tearing at meat, such as the carcass of a dead animal.

The shape of a bird's feet can tell you where a bird lives. A loon has webbed feet that allow it to dive and swim long distances underwater. A penguin doesn't fly, so it must rely on its feet for movement. The feet of a penguin are located close to its tail, allowing the penguin to walk upright on the ice where it lives.

1. What would be two headings you would use to describe the above section?

_____

2. Write a brief summary of the above selection.

_____

_____

_____

Harcourt

What Are Mammals and Birds?

Lesson Concept

Most mammals have fur or hair, and give birth to live young. Most birds have feathers and lay eggs from which young are hatched.

Vocabulary

mammals (A52)   **birds** (A55)

Match each phrase with the best answer. Write the letter of the best answer on the line. Some may have more than one answer.

_____ **1.** These are traits mammals share.

_____ **2.** Birds are grouped based on the shape of these features.

_____ **3.** These cover most of a bird's body.

A feathers
B fur or hair
C lungs to breathe
D usually give birth to live young
E beaks
F feed their young with milk made in their bodies
G feet

Label each mammal with an *M*. Label each bird with a *B*.

4. _____   5. _____   6. _____

7. _____   8. _____   9. _____

Harcourt

From Egg to Frog

Materials

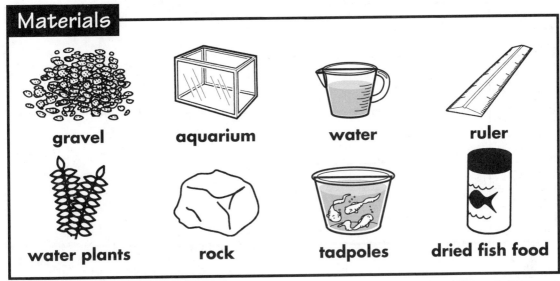

gravel   **aquarium**   **water**   **ruler**

water plants   **rock**   **tadpoles**   **dried fish food**

Activity Procedure

1 Put a layer of gravel on the bottom of the aquarium. Add 12 cm to 15 cm of water.

2 Float some water plants on top of the water, and stick others into the gravel. Add the rock. It should be big enough so that frogs can sit on it later and be out of the water.

3 Put two or three tadpoles, or young frogs, in the water. Put the aquarium where there is some light but no direct sunlight.

4 Feed the tadpoles a small amount of dried fish food once a day. Add fresh water to the aquarium once a week.

5 **Observe** the tadpoles every day. Once a week, make a drawing of what they look like. Use the charts below and on the next page for your data.

	Observations	Drawing
Day 1		
Day 2		
Day 3		
Day 4		
Day 5		

Harcourt

Name _____

	Observations	Drawing
Day 6		
Day 7		
Day 8		
Day 9		
Day 10		
Day 11		
Day 12		
Day 13		
Day 14		
Day 15		

Draw Conclusions

1. What changes did you see as the tadpoles grew? _____

_____

_____

2. When the tadpoles began to climb out of the water, what did their bodies

look like? _____

_____

3. Scientists at Work Scientists **record** what they **observe**. How did
recording your observations help you learn about the growing tadpoles?

_____

Investigate Further How important were the water plants to the growth
of the tadpoles? **Form a hypothesis** about this question, and **plan an
experiment** to test your hypothesis.

_____

_____

_____

Harcourt

Name _____

Date _____

Observe and Record

When you **observe** something, you use your senses of sight, hearing, smell, and touch. You can **record** your observations.

Think About Observing and Recording

Eva has a fish tank with tropical fish living in it. One day she notices that the glass sides of the tank have green matter on them. The filter is much too loud. An unpleasant smell is coming from the water. The side of the tank feels cold. She doesn't hear the hum of the heater that keeps the water warm.

1. Count how many times she used each of her senses in observing her fish tank. Record the numbers in the columns.

Sight	Hearing	Smell	Touch	Taste

2. **Record** what Eva saw.

    She saw: _____

3. **Record** what Eva heard (or did not hear).

    She heard: _____

    She missed hearing: _____

4. **Record** what Eva smelled, touched, and tasted.

    Smell: _____

    Touch: _____

    Taste: _____

5. Use all these observations to suggest what is wrong with the tank.

    _____

    _____

Harcourt

Name _____

Date _____

Reading Skills Practice

Arrange Events in Sequence

Sea Horses and Their Young

The following sentences describe how a sea horse reproduces. The sentences are out of sequence. Match the sentence with the number to show what you think the sequence should be. Then use some of the signal words in the box to rewrite the sentences in paragraph form.

1. The female sea horse deposits fertilized eggs into a special pouch of the male sea horse. The pouch is located near the tail of the sea horse. The eggs remain in the pouch until they are hatched.

2. The eggs hatch.

3. The young sea horses are pushed out through an opening in the pouch.

4. The sea horse is distinctive because the male, not the female, carries the eggs.

Signal Words:	first	next	finally

_____

_____

_____

_____

_____

_____

Harcourt

Use with page A61.

Name _____

Date _____

What Are Amphibians, Fish, and Reptiles?

Lesson Concept

Amphibians begin life in water, fish live all their lives in water, and reptiles are land animals.

Vocabulary

amphibians (A60)   **gills** (A61)   **fish** (A62)

scales (A62)   **reptiles** (A63)

Fill in each blank with a vocabulary term.

Animals that begin life in water, change in form, and then live on land are

called _____. _____ live in the

water, use _____ for breathing, and have body parts

that help them swim. _____ are land animals that are

covered with _____.

Label each animal as *amphibian, fish,* or *reptile*. Circle the animals that have gills at some time during their lives. Cross out the animals that always breathe with lungs.

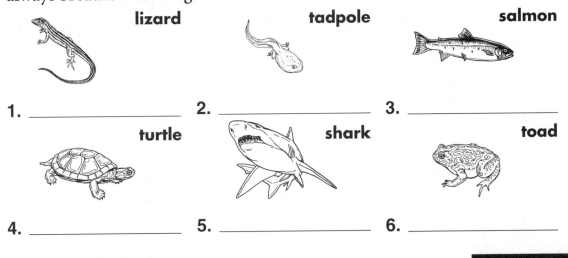

lizard   tadpole   salmon

1. _____   2. _____   3. _____

turtle   shark   toad

4. _____   5. _____   6. _____

Use with page A65.

Harcourt

How Animals Hide

Harcourt

Materials

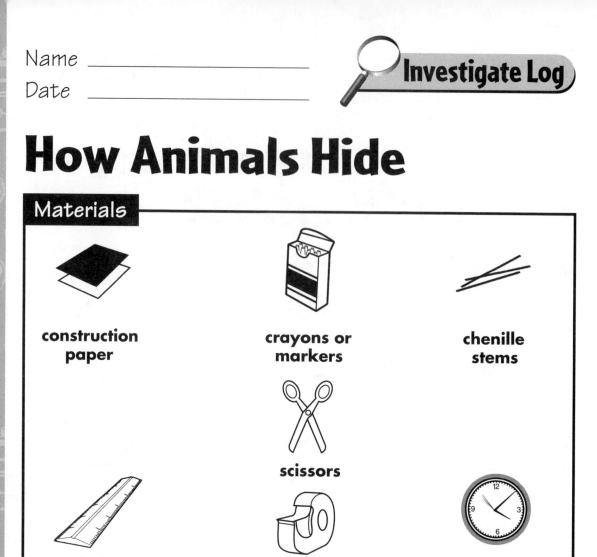

construction paper

crayons or markers

chenille stems

scissors

ruler

tape

watch or clock

Activity Procedure

1. Choose a place in the room to put your insect. Note the color and shape of objects in that place. Decide what color and shape your insect should be to blend in.

2. Your insect should be at least 5 cm long and 3 cm wide. Use a ruler to draw a rectangle this size. Draw the shape of your insects inside the rectangle. (Picture A)

3. Color your insect. Use colors and patterns that blend in with the place you chose for your insect.

4. Place your insect. It should be in full view and not hidden behind anything. If necessary, use tape to hold it in place. (Picture B)

5. When all the insects are placed, ask someone from another class to be a bird. Tell the "bird" to find as many insects as he or she can in one minute. Record in the chart the number found.

Investigate Log

6. Give the bird another minute to find more insects. Record the number found. Continue until all the insects have been found.

Minute	Number of Insects Found
1	
2	
3	

Draw Conclusions

1. Which insects were found first? How could they have been harder to find?

_____

_____

2. Which insects were found last? Why were they so hard to see?

_____

_____

3. Scientists at Work Scientists **observe** animals closely to see how they blend in with their environment. How did observing help you understand how insects' shapes and colors help them do this?

_____

_____

_____

_____

Name _____

Date _____

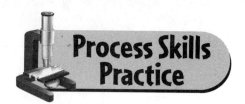

Make a Model

Scientists often make a model of a process or an object in nature. This helps them to closely **observe** processes or objects that usually could not be studied easily in nature.

Think About Making a Model

Animals often take on the color, shape, or pattern of their environment. Cut two pieces of paper 4 cm square. Color one with black stripes. Color the other with black dots of assorted sizes.

A   **B**

1. Place the rectangle that you have colored with a black-stripe pattern over the animal in Picture A and then over the animal in Picture B. Which animal does this pattern help hide? Why does this pattern work well with this environment?

_____

_____

_____

2. Place the rectangle that you have colored with a black-dot pattern over the animal in Picture A and then over the animal in Picture B. Which animal does this pattern help hide? Why does this pattern work well with this environment?

_____

_____

_____

Harcourt

Name _____

Date _____

Identify Cause and Effect

Bats in Winter

In some regions, insect-eating bats have trouble finding food in winter. Some make long-distance trips to warmer places. Others spend the winter hibernating in caves. The bat's body temperature drops during hibernation, which means that the animal needs less food. During the winter, when there are no insects available, the bat will live off its body fat.

Read the selection above, and then identify the causes and effects.

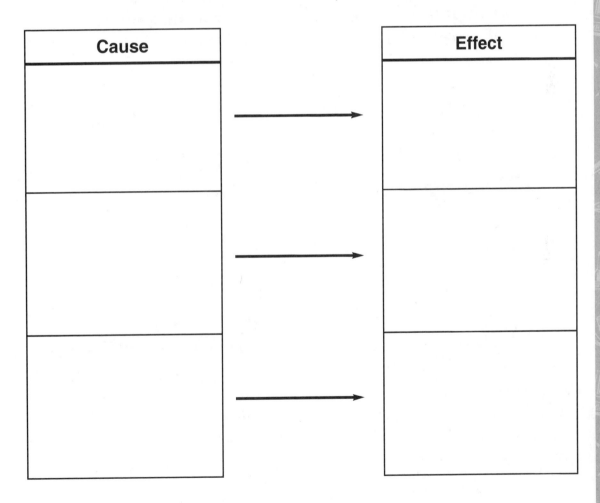

Cause	Effect

Harcourt

Concept Review

How Do Animals Behave?

Lesson Concept

Most animals have behavior that is both instinctive and learned. Some of these instincts help animals avoid danger. Write the word under each picture that describes the behavior of the animal.

Vocabulary

instinct (A68)
hibernate (A69)

migrate (A70)
camouflage (A72)
mimicry (A72)

_____   _____

_____   _____

_____

Harcourt

Use with page A73.

Name _____

Date _____

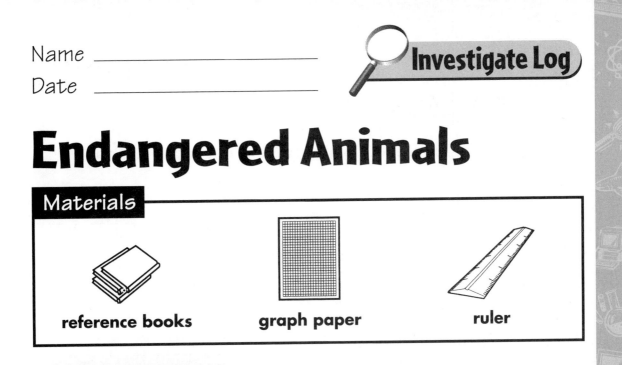

Endangered Animals

Materials

reference books   graph paper   ruler

Activity Procedure

1 Find a list of endangered species from reference books or the Internet.

2 Choose five endangered animals from the lists. Look for information about how the numbers of these animals have changed over time. Find out how many of each animal are living now.

3 Make a bar graph for your animals. For each animal, draw one bar to show how many were alive 10 years ago. Use a second bar to show how many are alive now.

4 Infer what will happen in the future to the animals on your graph. Explain your inferences, and share them with the class.

Harcourt

Name _____

Draw Conclusions

1. How did **using numbers** help you **organize your data** in this activity?

_____

_____

_____

2. What could happen that would change your **prediction**? **Record** your

ideas. _____

_____

3. **Scientists at Work** Scientists **use numbers** to help them **organize their data**. They then use their data to make inferences. How did making a bar graph help you make your prediction about the future of the animals?

_____

_____

_____

Investigate Further Animals are not the only kinds of organisms that can become endangered. Find information on five kinds of plants that are endangered, and make a bar graph as you did for the animals.

_____

_____

Harcourt

Name _____

Date _____

Use Numbers and Infer

When you use numbers, you can summarize and try to understand data in a table. When you infer, you form an opinion about what the numbers show. The opinion is called an inference.

Think About Inferring and Using Numbers

The table below shows the populations of wolves and deer in an area between 1900 and 1940. The wolf and deer populations stayed about the same before 1900. Then sheep farmers began killing the wolves. Without predators, the deer population started to increase. Review the information in the table. Then use it to answer the questions below.

	Wolf Population	**Deer Population**
1900	850	10,000
1910	500	15,000
1920	400	22,000
1930	100	27,000
1940	10	36,000

1. Use numbers to explain what happened to the deer population.

_____

2. Use numbers to explain what happened to the wolf population.

_____

3. What can you infer about why deer increased in population while wolves decreased? _____

_____

_____

Harcourt

Name _____

Date _____

Reading Skills Practice

Use Reference Sources

Use an encyclopedia or on-line resource to determine whether each of the following animals is threatened, endangered, or extinct.

Animal	Status
California Condor	
Snow Leopard	
Dodo	
Bald Eagle	
Passenger Pigeon	
Japanese Giant Salamander	

Choose an endangered species to research. Find out the causes of the animals endangerment and what is being done to protect this animal. Report your findings to the class.

_____

_____

_____

_____

_____

_____

Harcourt

Name _____

Date _____

What Is Extinction?

Harcourt

Lesson Concept

Sometimes animal species become extinct. Extinction can be natural. People can also cause extinction. Laws protect some animals that are in danger of becoming extinct.

Vocabulary

extinct (A76)   **endangered** (A76)   **fossil** (A77)

species (A76)   **threatened** (A77)

Underline the best answer.

1. Evidence of an animal or plant that lived long ago is a(n) ____.
   A fossil   **B** species   **C** organism   **D** rock

2. A ____ is a type of organism.
   A species   **B** habitat   **C** population   **D** fossil

3. A species that no longer exists is ____.
   A endangered   **B** threatened   **C** extinct   **D** growing

4. Most species become extinct today because their ____ is destroyed.
   A predator   **B** habitat   **C** food   **D** mate

5. A species that is in danger of becoming extinct is ____.
   A threatened   **B** endangered   **C** healthy   **D** stable

6. There are ____ to protect threatened and endangered animals.
   A predators   **B** species   **C** hunters   **D** laws

7. A species that is on its way to becoming endangered or extinct is ____.
   A threatened   **B** dead   **C** increasing   **D** fossilized

Name _____

Date _____

Vocabulary Review

Recognize Vocabulary

Match the definitions on the left with the terms on the right.

_____ **1.** animal that lives in water its whole life

_____ **2.** body parts that take in oxygen from the water

_____ **3.** animal that has fur or hair

_____ **4.** how animals get traits from their parents

_____ **5.** animal that has feathers, wings, and two legs

_____ **6.** land animal with dry skin, covered with scales

_____ **7.** animal that begins life in water and moves on to land as an adult

_____ **8.** a body feature an animal inherits

_____ **9.** small, thin, flat plates that help protect fish

_____ **10.** steadily going down in number

_____ **11.** evidence of an organism that lived long ago

_____ **12.** gone forever

_____ **13.** in danger of becoming extinct

_____ **14.** group of related organisms

A amphibian

B bird

C fish

D gills

E inherit

F mammal

G reptile

H scales

I trait

J species

K extinct

L threatened

M fossil

N endangered

Use with pages A40–A81.

Name _____

Date _____

Write Bird-Watching Field Notes

Informative Writing—Description

Imagine you are a bird-watcher who has sighted a new kind of bird. Draw a picture of the bird. Think of a name for the bird. Write a set of field notes describing the bird's traits. Use the outline below to help you plan your writing.

Drawing of Bird

Field Notes

Name of Bird: _____

Habitat: _____

Traits

Size: _____

Color: _____

Beak Shape: _____

Foot Shape: _____

Where It Nests: _____

Use with page A87.

Harcourt

Chapter 1 • Graphic Organizer for Chapter Concepts

Where Living Things Are Found

LESSON 1
WHAT ARE ECOSYSTEMS?

1. The environment

_____
_____

2. A population

_____
_____

3. A community

_____
_____

4. A habitat

_____
_____

LESSON 2
WHAT ARE FOREST ECOSYSTEMS?

1. A deciduous forest

_____
_____

2. A tropical rain forest

_____
_____

3. A coastal forest

_____
_____

4. A coniferous forest

_____
_____

LESSON 3
WHAT IS A DESERT ECOSYSTEM?

Hot and cold deserts

_____
_____
_____

LESSON 4
WHAT IS A GRASSLAND ECOSYSTEM?

1. Rainfall

_____
_____

2. Temperature

_____
_____

LESSON 5
WHAT ARE WATER ECOSYSTEMS?

1. Freshwater ecosystems

_____
_____
_____

2. Saltwater ecosystems

_____
_____

Harcourt

Observing an Environment

Materials

wire clothes hanger

Activity Procedure

1 Bend your hanger to make a square. Go outside and place the hanger on the ground. Inside this square is the environment you will **observe**.

2 Make a list of all the things you **observe** below. Next to each thing on your list, **record** whether it is living or nonliving. Write *L* for living and *N* for nonliving.

3 Ask a classmate to share his or her list with you. **Compare** the environments each of you observed.

4 Choose a living thing you **observed** in your hanger environment. Talk with a classmate about which things in the environment help the living thing survive.

_____   _____

_____   _____

_____   _____

_____   _____

_____   _____

Harcourt

Name _____

Draw Conclusions

1. Describe the environment you **observed**. _____

_____

_____

_____

_____

_____

2. How can you use **observation** to find out how an animal lives?

_____

_____

_____

_____

_____

3. Scientists at Work Scientists learn by **observing** and by **gathering data**. They also learn from the data gathered by others. What did you learn about an environment from your classmate's data?

_____

_____

_____

_____

_____

Investigate Further Observe a sample of soil in which an earthworm lives. Describe the environment. **Predict** what would happen if all the earthworms disappeared. _____

_____

_____

_____

_____

Harcourt

Name _____

Date _____

Observing and Gathering Data

During experiments, you collect measurements like times and temperatures. At the end of the experiment, you arrange these measurements to make it easier to interpret the data.

Think About Observing and Gathering Data

Three third-grade classes in three different schools did a joint bug-observing project. Each class observed an environment once a week for four weeks. The classes gathered data and recorded their observations. Class 1 observed ants and an anthill on the playground next to the kindergarten sandbox. The students used a hand lens to observe the ants. Class 2 observed yellow banana slugs under a barrel in the woods next to their school. Class 3 found a caterpillar on a tree and observed it. Fill in the chart below with the classes' observations.

	Environment	Nonliving Things	Living Things
Class 1			
Class 2			
Class 3			

1. What do you think you can learn about a living thing by observing it?

_____

2. Why do you think Class 1 used a hand lens to observe the ants?

_____

_____

Harcourt

Predict Possible Future Outcomes

The Flood

Jason and his family live on a small street. Many families and their pets live in homes on the street. A stream flows behind their houses. Animals such as ducks, fish, frogs, and insects make their homes in and near the stream. Deer often come to drink the water from the stream and eat the berries from the plants that grow there. Birds make nests in the tall trees. One spring it rained so much that the water in the stream spilled over its banks and flooded the street, the homes, and the entire area near the stream. The flood remained for many days before the water returned to its normal level.

Write a paragraph below that predicts how all the living things might have been affected by the flood.

_____

_____

_____

_____

_____

_____

_____

_____

Use with page B8.

Harcourt

Name _____

Date _____

What Are Ecosystems?

Lesson Concept

The living and nonliving things that interact and affect each other form an ecosystem.

Vocabulary

environment (B6)   **ecosystem** (B7)   **population** (B7)

community (B7)   **habitat** (B7)

Underline the best answer.

1. A large number of frogs are spotted in a pond. All the frogs in the ecosystem are ____.

   A a habitat   **B** an ecosystem   **C** a population

2. Other living things live in the pond. All the living things in the ecosystem are ____.

   A a habitat   **B** an environment   **C** a community

3. A ____ provides for the needs of the groups living in the pond.

   A population   **B** habitat   **C** ecosystem

4. Draw an ecosystem in the aquarium below. Make a habitat of water, rocks, and plants. Add a population of fish.

Harcourt

Variety in Forests

Materials

tray of beans, labeled "Tray 1"

tray of beans, labeled "Tray 2"

2 paper cups

Activity Procedure

1 Tray 1 stands for the trees in a tropical rain forest. Tray 2 stands for the trees in a deciduous forest. Each kind of bean stands for a different kind of tree.

2 Scoop a cupful of beans from each tray. Carefully pour each cup of beans into its own pile.

3 Work with a partner. One partner should work with the beans from Tray 1. The other partner should work with the beans from Tray 2.

4 Sort the beans into groups so that each group contains only one kind of bean.

5 **Record** a description of each type of bean in the data table below. Count the number of beans in each small pile. Record these numbers in the data table.

Tropical Rain Forest (Tray 1)		Deciduous Forest (Tray 2)	
Kind of Bean	**Number of Beans**	**Kind of Bean**	**Number of Beans**

Name _____

Draw Conclusions

1. How many kinds of "trees" were in each "forest"? _____

_____

_____

_____

2. Which forest had the most trees of one kind? Why do you think this

was so? _____

_____

_____

_____

3. **Scientists at Work** Scientists learn by **gathering, recording,** and
interpreting data. What did you learn from your data about variety

in forests? _____

_____

_____

_____

Investigate Further Suppose you want to find out what kinds of trees are
most common in your community. Explain how you could **use numbers** to

find out. _____

_____

_____

Harcourt

Name _____

Date _____

Process Skills Practice

Use Numbers

Using numbers is one way to gather information and record data from an investigation. You can draw a conclusion based on the data you collect.

Think About Using Numbers

Roger lives on a farm. He writes to his pen pal, Teresa, "Our apple trees are doing well this year. We are taking lots of apples to the farmers' market every Tuesday." Teresa writes back, "I live in the city. I've never ever seen an apple tree. How many apples do you take to the market on one day?" Roger goes out into the barn. He sees apples in boxes, piled high. He doesn't want to count every one. He reads the side of one of the boxes and sees that there are 50 apples in each box. He writes that number in his notebook. He counts the boxes. There are 10. Roger writes to Teresa, "We are taking 500 apples to the market this week!"

Apples: 50 in each box
Boxes: 10

1. Why do you think Roger didn't want to count each apple? _____

_____

2. What did Roger want to investigate? _____

_____

3. What data did Roger gather and record? _____

_____

4. What conclusion did Roger come to? _____

_____

5. How do you think Roger used numbers to come to this conclusion?

_____

_____

Harcourt

Use with page B13.

Name _____

Date _____

Summarize and Paraphrase a Selection

Rain Forest

A tropical rain forest is hot and wet all year. The average yearly temperature in a tropical rain forest is 30°C. The average yearly rainfall is 180 centimeters. A wide variety of plants and animals live in the three layers of the rain forest. The top layer of the rain forest, called the canopy, gets lots of water and sunlight. Many animals drink water that collects on the leaves. Orchids, mosses, and ferns grow on the trunks of tall trees in the middle layer of the rain forest, called the understory. The lowest layer of the rain forest, which is called the forest floor, gets very little sunlight.

Write four sentences to summarize the paragraph.

_____

_____

_____

_____

What might be three subheadings you could use in this paragraph?

_____   _____   _____

Harcourt

Name _____

Date _____

Concept Review

What Are Forest Ecosystems?

Lesson Concept

There are four main forest ecosystems. These forests provide habitats for plants and animals.

Vocabulary

deciduous forest (B15)   **forest** (B14)   **coastal forest** (B17)

coniferous forest (B18)   **tropical rain forest** (B16)

Fill in the blanks below with vocabulary terms from above.

A forest is an area in which the main plants are trees. One kind of forest where the trees have large, flat leaves that drop in the fall is called a

_____. A _____ grows in places that are hot and wet all year. That kind of forest has trees that grow very tall and have leaves that stay green all year. A _____ grows where there is a lot of rain, and where it does not get too warm or too cold.

The trees in a _____ form seeds in cones.

1. In which kind of forest would you find this tree?

_____

2. List the three layers of a tropical rain forest.

_____   _____   _____

3. How does the triangle shape of conifers protect them?

_____

_____

Harcourt

Name _____

Date _____

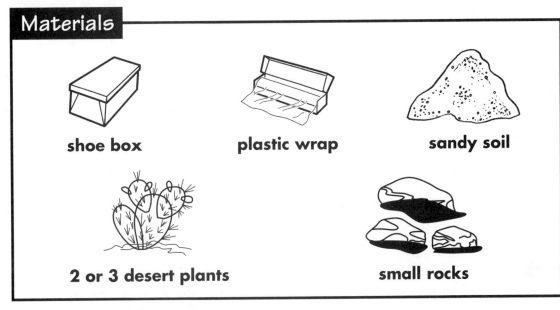

Investigate Log

Make a Desert Ecosystem

Materials

shoe box

plastic wrap

sandy soil

2 or 3 desert plants

small rocks

Activity Procedure

1 **Make a model** of a desert ecosystem. Start by lining the shoe box with plastic wrap. Place sandy soil in the shoe box. Make sure the soil is deep enough for the plants.

2 Place the plants in the soil, and place the rocks around them. Lightly sprinkle the soil with water.

3 Place your desert ecosystem in a sunny location.

4 Every two or three days, use your finger to **observe** how dry the soil is. If the soil is *very* dry, add a small amount of water. If the soil is damp, do not add water. Be careful not to water the plants too much.

5 Continue to **observe** and care for your desert ecosystem. **Record** what you observe.

My Observations: _____

_____

_____

_____

Harcourt

Name _____

Draw Conclusions

1. What kind of environment does your desert ecosystem model?

   _____

   _____

2. How does **making a model** help you learn about a desert?

   _____

   _____

3. **Scientists at Work** Scientists often learn by **making models.** What other

   types of ecosystems can you make models of? _____

   _____

Investigate Further How would getting rain every day change a desert
ecosystem? **Plan an experiment** in which you could **use a model** to find out.

_____

_____

_____

Harcourt

Name _____

Date _____

Make a Model

Sometimes you may want to observe something that is very large.
You can make a small model and observe the model instead.

Think About Making a Model

You live in a climate that is hot and dry in the summer and cold and rainy
in the winter. Suppose you make a model of a desert ecosystem in the backyard of your home. You make it during the hottest part of the summer. You
plant some desert plants in sandy soil. Each day the blazing sun shines on your
ecosystem. You give the plants a few drops of water once a week. The plants
grow well. Then, when the summer is over, your ecosystem begins to change.

1. What is the purpose of a model? _____

_____

_____

2. What does this model teach you? _____

_____

3. What do you think will happen to your model at the end of the summer?

_____

_____

_____

_____

4. Draw a picture of the backyard desert ecosystem.

Harcourt

Name _____

Date _____

Use Graphic Sources for Information

Desert Animals

Use the pictures to help you answer the questions.

1. How does the snake keep cool in the hot desert?

_____

2. How does the bird get water?

_____

3. How does the lizard keep warm at night?

_____

4. Name one animal that is active during the night.

_____

Use with page B23.

What Is a Desert Ecosystem?

Lesson Concept

A desert is an ecosystem found in areas that get very little rainfall.

Vocabulary

desert (B22)

Underline the best answer.

1. Hot deserts can have temperatures of over ___ during the day.

   A 23°C (about 73° F) **B** 43°C (about 110° F)

2. The Taklimakan desert in China has ___ in the winter.

   A freezing temperatures and blizzards **B** notably high temperatures

3. The barrel cactus has parts that allow it to live in hot deserts. The barrel cactus does NOT have ___.

   A a thick skin **B** very deep roots **C** a thick stem **D** very shallow roots

4. Desert animals get most of their water from eating plants or ___.

   A fruits **B** vegetables **C** other animals **D** nuts

5. You want to observe rabbits in the desert. Should you look for them during the day or during the night? Explain. _____

   _____

   _____

Harcourt

Grass Roots

Materials

trowel   paper   hand lens

Activity Procedure

1. **CAUTION** **Make sure you have permission to dig in the spot you choose.** Dig out a small clump of grass, about the size of your palm. Be sure to include the roots.

2. Hold up the clump of grass. **Observe** what happens to the soil around the roots. Gently shake the grass, and again **observe** the soil around the roots.

3. Carefully remove the soil from the roots, and separate one grass plant from the rest.

4. Put the grass plant on a clean sheet of paper. **Observe** it with the hand lens. The leaves of a grass plant are called blades. Notice how the roots and blades are shaped.

5. Draw your grass plant. Label the roots and blades.

Harcourt

Name _____

Draw Conclusions

1. Describe the roots of grass plants. How might they help hold soil in place?

_____

_____

_____

2. Think about the leaves of other plants. How do grass blades **compare** with the leaves of other plants?

_____

_____

_____

3. Scientists at Work Scientists make inferences about plants by closely **observing** them. The blades of grass plants do not lose much water to the air around them. Grass roots can absorb water from large areas of soil. From these facts, **infer** the kinds of places in which many grasses live.

_____

_____

_____

Investigate Further Take a walk in the neighborhood. Look for places where the soil has been washed away. **Observe** the slope of the land and the plants growing in those places. **Form a hypothesis** about how to prevent more soil from washing away. Share your hypothesis with your class.

Harcourt

Observe and Infer

When you **observe**, you use your senses to find out what is happening. You then can use what you have observed to **infer** an opinion or an explanation.

Think About Observing and Inferring

Suppose that you take a trip to another state. While you are there, you notice that the grass is very dry and brown. You remember that the grass where you live is soft and green.

1. What did you **observe** about the grass in the place you are visiting?

_____

2. What did you **observe** about the grass where you live?

_____

3. What are some possible reasons that the grass in the place you are visiting is dry and brown?

_____

_____

_____

4. From the reasons you gave in Question 3, choose one and write a sentence stating what you have **inferred** about why the grass is dry and brown.

_____

_____

_____

5. What is one way to find out whether your inference is correct?

_____

_____

Harcourt

Use with page B27.

Name _____

Date _____

Compare and Contrast

Deserts and Grasslands

Deserts and grasslands are two types of ecosystems that you have studied. Deserts have very little rainfall—often less than 25 centimeters of rain each year. Grasslands, on the other hand, average 30 to 60 centimeters of rain each year. There are hot deserts and cold deserts. Plants that grow in deserts are adapted to the dryness. They have parts that help them save water. Their roots are long and shallow. They spread out near the top of the soil and soak up the water when it rains. Grasslands are found where it is hot during the summer and cold during the winter. They are large, flat areas of land that are covered with grass. Many animals live in the desert. They get most of their water by eating plants that store water or by eating other animals. Many of the animals sleep during the day and hunt for food at night. The grassland is home to many animals. Because there is no place to hide in the grassland, many animals burrow under the ground. Some animals are good runners and escape their predators by getting away. Today many grasslands have become farms, ranches, and towns.

Use the information in the selection to compare and contrast deserts and grasslands.

1. How are deserts and grasslands alike? _____

_____

_____

2. Compare the amount of rainfall in deserts and grasslands.

_____

_____

3. Why do you think grasslands have become farms, ranches, and towns?

_____

_____

_____

_____

Harcourt

Name _____

Date _____

Grasslands

Grasslands are large areas in which there is enough water for grass to grow but not enough water to support the growth of trees.

Vocabulary

grassland (B28)

Place a check mark in front of the sentence in each pair that is a fact about grasslands.

1. ____Grasslands have lots of grass, trees, shrubs, and wildflowers.
   ____Grasslands have lots of grass but few, if any, trees.

2. ____Grasslands receive about as much rainfall as deserts.
   ____Grasslands receive more rainfall than deserts.

3. ____Grasslands are large, flat areas.
   ____Grasslands are small, hilly areas.

4. ____Grasslands are found in only a few areas of the United States and nowhere else.
   ____Grasslands are found in many places around the world.

5. ____Grasslands are also called *mountains* or *deserts*.
   ____Grasslands are also called *pampas* or *steppes*.

6. ____Many different types of animals live in grasslands.
   ____Very few animals live in grasslands.

7. ____Many animals in grasslands make their homes from sticks and twigs.
   ____Many animals in grasslands make their homes in underground burrows.

Harcourt

Use with page B31.

Name _____

Date _____

Make a Freshwater Ecosystem

Materials

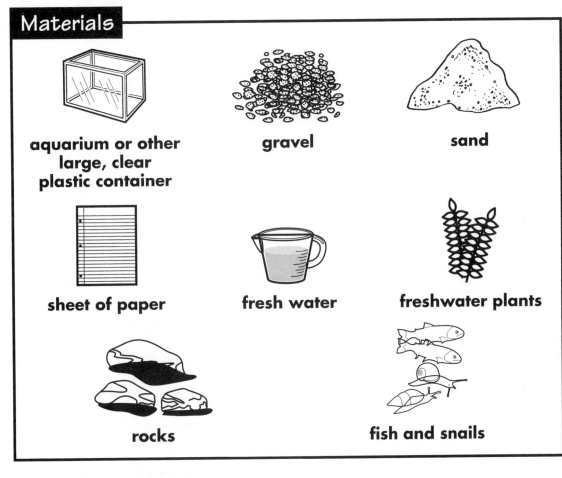

aquarium or other large, clear plastic container

gravel

sand

sheet of paper

fresh water

freshwater plants

rocks

fish and snails

Activity Procedure

1 Put a layer of gravel at the bottom of the tank. Add a layer of sand on top of the gravel.

2 Set the aquarium in a place where it isn't too sunny. Place a sheet of paper over the sand. Slowly add the water to the tank. Make sure you pour the water onto the paper so the sand will stay in place.

3 Remove the paper, and put the plants and rocks into the tank. Let the tank sit for about one week. After one week, add the fish and snails.

4 **Observe** and care for your freshwater ecosystem.

Harcourt

Name _____

Draw Conclusions

1. What are some things you **observed** in your freshwater ecosystem?

_____

_____

_____

_____

2. Why do you think you waited to add the fish to the tank?

_____

_____

_____

_____

_____

3. **Scientists at Work** Scientists often **make a model** of an ecosystem so they can **observe** it in a laboratory. How did making a model help you observe a freshwater ecosystem? How is your model different from a real pond?

_____

_____

_____

_____

Investigate Further What other kinds of plants and animals might live in a freshwater ecosystem? To find out, visit a pet shop that sells fish. Make a list of the freshwater plants and animals you find there. _____

_____

_____

_____

_____

Harcourt

Name _____

Date _____

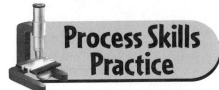

Make a Model

You can make a model to observe something that would be difficult to observe in the classroom. When you make a model, you have to be careful, or your model won't work.

Think About Making a Model

Jeff made a model of a freshwater ecosystem. He put a layer of gravel on the bottom of a large, clear plastic container. He added a layer of sand. He poured water into the tank. The sand would not stay in place. It clouded the water. He had to start again. He put paper over the sand and poured the water in. He set his plants and rocks on top of the paper. When he saw what he had done, he had to take the plants and rocks out again. He took the paper off. Then he put the plants and rocks into the tank. He added the fish and snails right away. The fish did not look well. He took them out and put them back in his other aquarium. He let the water sit for a week. He added the fish and snails. They did well.

1. What mistakes did Jeff make in his model of a freshwater ecosystem?

_____

_____

_____

2. Infer why the fish and snails did not do well when Jeff put them in the

tank without waiting a week. _____

_____

_____

3. Write the correct steps for making a model of a freshwater ecosystem.

_____

_____

_____

_____

Harcourt

Compare and Contrast

Water Ecosystems

freshwater	saltwater	ocean	lake	salt
tide pool	barnacles	American egret	river	

Fill in the blanks using the words above.

In a _____ ecosystem, the water contains very little salt. In a _____

ecosystem, the water has a lot of _____. An example of a saltwater ecosystem

is an _____. An example of a freshwater ecosystem is a _____. A _____

_____ is a saltwater ecosystem that forms at an ocean shoreline. _____

are small animals that live there. A _____ is a freshwater ecosystem that is

usually larger and deeper than a pond. An _____ is a wading bird

that might make its home near a pond.

**Write a sentence that tells how freshwater and saltwater ecosystems
are similar.** _____

_____

Name _____

Date _____

What Are Water Ecosystems?

Lesson Concept

Water ecosystems may have salt water or fresh water.

Vocabulary

salt water (B34)	**fresh water** (B34)

Underline the best answer.

1. You go on a field trip to the aquarium. It is near the ocean. You see a display of a kelp forest. It is 10 meters (about 30 ft) deep. Which ecosystem are you looking at?

   A freshwater   **B** saltwater

2. A beach is right outside the aquarium. Shallow salt water collects in the middle of some big rocks on the beach. The sun warms the water. Many plants and animals live in the warm, shallow water. What is the correct name for this area?

   A pond   **B** river   **C** tide pool   **D** kelp forest

3. At the aquarium, you see a movie about ecosystems. People are swimming. When the people finish swimming, you see how still the water is. You see turtles crawling at the edge of the water. What kind

   of ecosystem is this? How do you know? _____

   _____

   _____

Name _____

Date _____

Recognize Vocabulary

In the space provided, write the letter of the term in Column B that best fits the definition in Column A. Use each term only once.

Column A

_____ **1.** a forest that contains mostly evergreens

_____ **2.** an ecosystem found in areas that get very little rainfall

_____ **3.** water that has lots of salt in it

_____ **4.** an area in which the main plants are trees

_____ **5.** everything around a living thing

_____ **6.** provides a population with all its needs

_____ **7.** a forest mostly made up of trees that drop their leaves each fall

_____ **8.** water that has very little salt in it

_____ **9.** a forest that grows in places that are hot and wet all year

_____ **10.** living and nonliving things interacting in an environment

_____ **11.** a group of the same kind of living things that live in the same place at the same time

_____ **12.** a forest that grows where it does not get too warm or too cold and where there is a lot of rain

_____ **13.** all the populations that live in an ecosystem

Column B

A fresh water

B coniferous forest

C desert

D environment

E ecosystem

F tropical rain forest

G coastal forest

H salt water

I forest

J population

K community

L deciduous forest

M habitat

Harcourt

Name _____

Date _____

Write a Web Page

Persuasive Writing–Request

Imagine that you work for a group that wants to protect desert ecosystems. Write three paragraphs for the group's Web page. Tell readers about the animals and plants that live in the desert. Ask people not to do things that can damage the desert ecosystem. Use the outline below to help you plan your Web page.

Paragraph 1
Animals and plants that live in the desert

Paragraph 2
Things that can damage the desert ecosystem

Paragraph 3
Reasons people should not damage the desert ecosystem

Harcourt

Chapter 2 • Graphic Organizer for Chapter Concepts

Living Things Depend on One Another

LESSON 1   HOW DO LIVING THINGS GET FOOD?

They _____ with their environment to get _____ .

_____ interact with sunlight, air, and water to make their own food.

Animals are _____ . They eat other living things.

eat other living things that have died.

LESSON 2   MODELS OF THESE INTERACTIONS ARE _____ ,

which show how food and energy move from one living thing to another.

which shows how energy decreases at each level of the food chain.

LESSON 3   WHICH IN TURN LEAD TO FOOD WEBS

A food web is made of _____ .

Members of the Food Web Are _____ ,

which are animals that hunt and eat other animals.

which are animals that are hunted and used as food.

Harcourt

Animal Teeth

Materials

blank index cards   books about animals

Activity Procedure

1 **Observe** the pictures of the animals. Look closely at the shape of each animal's teeth.

2 Use one index card for each animal. **Record** the animal's name, and draw the shape of its teeth.

3 With a partner, make a list of words that describe the teeth. **Record** these words next to the drawings on the index cards.

4 Think about the things each animal eats. Use books about animals if you need help. On the back of each index card, make a list of the things the animal eats.

Harcourt

Name _____

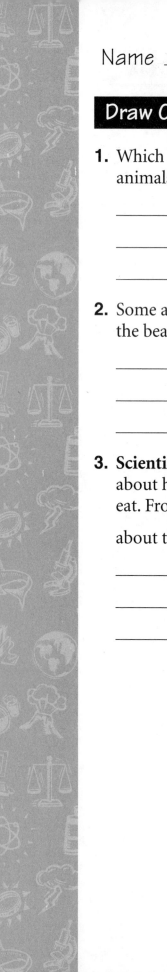
Draw Conclusions

1. Which animals might use their teeth to catch other animals? Which animals might use their teeth to eat plants? Explain.

_____

_____

_____

2. Some animals use their teeth to help them do other things, too. **Observe** the beaver's teeth. How do its teeth help it cut down trees?

_____

_____

_____

3. Scientists at Work Scientists learn by **observing**. Scientists can learn about how animals use their teeth by watching how and what the animals eat. From what you observed in this investigation, what can you **infer**

about the shapes of animals' teeth? _____

_____

_____

Name _____

Date _____

Observe and Infer

When you observe, you use your senses. When you infer, you form an opinion based on what you have observed.

Think About Observing and Inferring

Your class goes on a field trip to a natural history museum. You see a display of wolves in their natural habitat. You observe that these animals have very sharp front teeth. In another display you see pictures of a dairy farm. You learn that cows have flat, grinding teeth. The final display shows the 32 teeth of an adult person. You learn that the front teeth are for cutting food, and the teeth next to them are sharp for ripping. The teeth way in the back have a fairly flat surface for grinding food.

1. Think about the cow's teeth. What inference can you make about what

cows eat? _____

_____

_____

2. What inference could you make about the purpose of a person's front

teeth? _____

3. From your observations of animal teeth, make up an imaginary animal.
Let it be an animal that eats only plants. Draw a picture showing the

teeth of the animal. Explain what the animal eats. _____

_____

_____

Harcourt

Name _____

Date _____

Identify Cause and Effect

Read the sentences below. In each sentence, underline the cause and circle the effect.

1. A carrot plant uses energy from the sun to make its own food.

2. As an earthworm feeds, it helps clean the environment.

3. A hungry rabbit eats a carrot for energy.

Read the paragraph, looking for causes and effects. Then finish the chart with three causes and effects found in the paragraph.

   A farmer planted a crop of corn. After getting a lot of sunlight and water, the corn plants grew very tall. Just before harvest, hungry crows flew into the field and started eating the corn. The farmer did not want the crows in his field because he was afraid they would ruin his crop. The farmer made two large scarecrows and placed them in the middle of the cornfield. The crows stopped coming to eat the corn. The farmer harvested the corn crop and sold most of the corn by the bushel. The farmer used the rest of the corn to feed his family.

Cause	Effect

Harcourt

Use with page B52.

How Do Animals Get Food?

Lesson Concept

Plants and animals depend on their environment and on one another to get the food they need.

Vocabulary

interact (B50) **herbivore** (B51) **producer** (B51)
consumer (B51) **carnivore** (B52) **decomposer** (B52)
　　　　　　　　　　omnivore (B52)

As you read the summary, fill in each blank with a vocabulary term from above. Answer the questions that follow.

Plants and animals work together, or _____ with the

environment to get what they need. Plants are _____.

They make their own food. Animals are _____. They

must eat plants or other animals. A _____ is a living
thing that breaks down once-living things for food.

Make a check mark in front of the statements that agree with your reading.

_____ All living things need food.

_____ Plants interact with sunlight, air, and water to make food.

_____ Animals that hunt and kill their food have body parts that help them get their food.

_____ Omnivores eat both plants and animals.

_____ Carnivores eat plants.

_____ Herbivores eat animals.

Use with page B53.

Make a Food-Chain Model

Materials

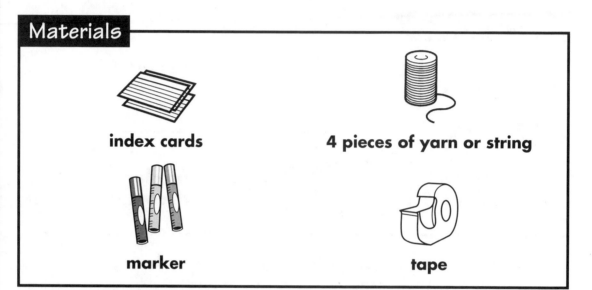

index cards

4 pieces of yarn or string

marker

tape

Activity Procedure

1 In the bottom right-hand corners, number the index cards 1 through 5.

2 On Card 1, draw and label grass. On Card 2, draw and label a cricket. On Card 3, draw and label a frog. On Card 4, draw and label a snake. On Card 5, draw and label a hawk.

3 Order the cards in a line with Card 1 first and Card 5 last. Use yarn and tape to connect the cards.

4 Stretch the connected cards out on a table. The cards form a model called a food chain.

5 Discuss with a classmate how each living thing in the food chain gets its food. Tell which things in your model show producers. Tell which things show consumers.

Harcourt

Draw Conclusions

1. In your model, which living thing is last in the food chain? Why do you think it is in this place? _____

_____

2. In which part of the food chain is the producer found? Why do you think it is there? _____

_____

_____

3. Scientists at Work Scientists **use models** to help them study things in nature. How does using a model of a food chain help you understand living things and the food they eat? _____

_____

_____

Name _____

Date _____

Make a Model

Using a model helps you learn about something you cannot observe in real life.

Think About Making a Model

You can make a model of a food chain by using the chart below. Write the names of these animals and plants in the correct columns: a whale; a pelican, which is a bird that eats fish; a small fish; and an ocean plantlike living thing called algae. Fill in the chart as you answer the questions.

Producers	Consumers	Food Chain

Fill in the chart as you answer the questions.

1. What would you list in the *Consumers* column? _____

_____

2. What is a consumer? _____

_____

_____

3. What would you list in the *Producers* column? _____

4. What is a producer? _____

_____

5. In the *Food Chain* column, list the four living things from the paragraph. Write the number *1* next to the living thing or things at the top of the food chain. Number the other living things to show their order in the food chain.

Harcourt

Use with page B55.

Name _____

Date _____

Arrange Events in Sequence

These sentences are out of order. Reorder the sentences to write a paragraph describing the food chain.

A zebra is a consumer that eats grass.

The stored food contains energy.

As the zebra eats the grass, it takes in energy.

The plants make and store their own food.

All plants are producers.

A lion is also a consumer, eating zebras for energy.

_____

_____

_____

_____

_____

_____

_____

_____

Harcourt

 **Concept Review**

What Are Food Chains?

Lesson Concept

A food chain is the path of food in an ecosystem from one living thing to another.

Vocabulary

food chain (B56) **energy pyramid** (B58)

Read the summary, and fill in the blanks with vocabulary terms from above.

All living things need energy to live. Living things get their energy from food. Producers get energy from sunlight and store energy in the food they make. Animals cannot make their own food, so they eat other living things.

A _____ shows how energy moves through the

environment. An _____ is a model that shows how the amount of energy in an ecosystem goes down for each higher animal in the food chain.

1. Underline the correct answer. A rabbit nibbles on grass. A bird eats a worm. Both animals are ____, which get energy from the food they eat.

consumers   producers   observers   meat-eaters

2. Put the stages of this food chain in the correct order by numbering each living thing with a 1, 2, 3, or 4, beginning with the blades of grass.

_____   _____   _____   _____

3. Suppose you have a peanut butter and jelly sandwich for lunch. Do the fillings of your sandwich come from producers or consumers?

_____

Harcourt

Make a Food Web

Materials

index cards, cut into fourths

poster board

tape or glue

crayons

Activity Procedure

1 Write the name of each living thing from the chart on the next page on its own card.

2 Glue the cards onto a sheet of poster board so they form a circle. Leave room for writing.

3 Look at the chart again. List two different food chains you could make.

4 Draw arrows between the parts of each food chain. Use a different color for each food chain. You have now made a food web.

5 **Observe** your model to see how the food chains overlap. What other living things could you add to your food web?

Harcourt

Living Thing	What It Eats
clover	uses the sun to make its own food
grasshopper	clover
frog	grasshopper
snake	frog, mouse
owl	snake
mouse	clover

Draw Conclusions

1. What is the producer in this food web? _____

2. What does your food web tell you about producers and consumers?

_____

_____

3. Scientists at Work Scientists sometimes **make models** to help them learn about things. How did drawing a food web help you learn about animals

in a real ecosystem? _____

_____

_____

Investigate Further Cut out magazine pictures of different plants and animals. Work with a partner to make a food web that includes these plants and animals.

Harcourt

Name _____

Date _____

Use a Model

When you make a model, you can learn about something that is hard to observe, such as a real-life food web.

Think About Using a Model

Chris visited the wetland near her house. She wrote down some of the things she saw. Some fish splashed in the stream. Caterpillars in the trees munched on new leaves. One fell into the water and was eaten by a fish. A bird swooped down into the water and came out again with a fish in its beak. Grubs crawled on the tree, chewing at the tree's bark. Another bird appeared and picked up one of the grubs in its beak. Chris made drawings of each of the things she saw. She cut out her drawings and glued them to a piece of cardboard. She drew arrows to connect the living things. Now she had a food web. After that, Chris sat down and ate a fish sandwich for lunch. Then she drew a picture of herself and added it to the food web.

1. What is the producer in this food web? _____

2. What are the consumers in this food web? _____

_____

3. List the different food chains in the food web. _____

_____

_____

4. Why did Chris put herself on the food web? _____

_____

5. Make a food web of the different food chains you are a part of.

Harcourt

Name _____

Date _____

Use Graphic Sources for Information

Look at the food web for this freshwater ecosystem. Finish the
chart showing the food source or sources for each living thing.

Living Thing	Food Source

Use with page B64.

Name _____

Date _____

What Are Food Webs?

Lesson Concept

A food web is a model that shows how food chains overlap and link together.

Vocabulary

food web (B62)	predator (B62)	prey (B62)

Look at the food web. Answer the questions that follow.

1. What is a predator? _____

2. Which of the animals on the food web are predators?

_____

3. What is prey? _____

4. Which of the animals are prey? _____

5. How can an animal, like the frog, be both predator and prey?

_____

_____

Harcourt

Recognize Vocabulary

Use the terms below to complete each sentence. The capital
letters will spell a hidden word. Unscramble the capital letters
to spell out the hidden word.

decompoSer	energy pyraMid	foOd chain
food wEb	conSumer	preY
produCer	prEdator	interacT

1. An animal that hunts another animal is called a _____.

2. A model that shows how energy is lost for each higher animal in a food

chain is called an _____.

3. The path of food from one living thing to another is a

_____.

4. An animal that is hunted is called _____.

5. Overlapping food chains are called a _____.

6. A living thing that breaks down the wastes of another living thing is a

_____.

7. When plants and animals work together, they _____.

8. A living thing that eats other living things is a _____.

9. A living thing that makes its own food is a _____.

Hidden Word: All plants and animals interact together to form an

emoyestsc. _____

Name _____

Date _____

Explain an Energy Pyramid

Informative Writing–Explanation

Choose one ecosystem. Write a paragraph that explains the energy pyramid for that ecosystem. To help you gather your ideas, draw and label the energy pyramid below for your ecosystem.

Ecosystem _____

Harcourt

Name _____ Date _____

Minerals, Rocks, and Fossils

LESSON 1
MINERALS AND ROCKS

Mineral Properties

1. _____
2. _____
3. _____

Mineral Uses

4. _____
5. _____
6. _____
7. _____

Rocks

8. made of _____

LESSON 2
HOW ROCKS FORM

Three Kinds of Rocks

1. _____
2. _____
3. _____

How Rocks Change
in the Rock Cycle

4. _____
5. _____
6. _____

Uses of Rocks

7. _____
8. _____
9. _____

LESSON 3
FOSSILS

Types of Fossils

1. _____
2. _____
3. _____
4. _____

What Fossils Show

5. _____

Testing Minerals

Materials

Minerals labeled A through G

Activity Procedure

1. Use the chart below.

2. A harder mineral scratches a softer mineral. Try to scratch each of the other minerals with Sample A. **Record** which minerals Sample A scratches.

3. A softer mineral is scratched by a harder mineral. Try to scratch Sample A with each of the other minerals. **Record** which minerals scratch Sample A.

4. Repeat Steps 2 and 3 for each mineral.

5. Using the information in your chart, **order** the minerals from softest to hardest. Give each mineral a number, starting with 1 for the softest mineral.

Mineral to Test	Minerals It Scratches	Minerals that Scratch It
Sample A		
Sample B		
Sample C		
Sample D		
Sample E		
Sample F		
Sample G		

Harcourt

Name _____

Investigate Log

Draw Conclusions

1. Which mineral was the hardest? _____

Which was the softest? _____

How do you know? _____

_____

_____

2. How did you decide the **order** of the minerals? _____

_____

_____

3. Scientists at Work Scientists often put objects in **order**. How can
putting minerals in order of hardness help you identify them?

_____

_____

Investigate Further To test for hardness, scientists sometimes scratch an
unknown mineral with common objects. That's because they don't always
have other minerals with them. But to use common objects, scientists
need to know how hard the objects are. Using the minerals from this
investigation, find out the hardness of glass, a copper penny, and your
fingernail. Put them in **order** with the minerals you tested.

Harcourt

Name _____

Date _____

Observe and Order

Think About Observing and Ordering

Stanley wants to make a display of rocks to bring to class. He goes on a rock-collecting walk. He needs to decide how to order the rocks. He observes the rocks. He sees that the rocks are different colors. There are pink, black, gray, and white rocks. Then he observes that some of the rocks are large and some are medium sized and some are small. There are also different-shaped rocks in his collection.

1. What are three observations Stanley can make about the rocks?

_____

_____

_____

2. Which sense was used to make those observations? _____

3. How could Stanley order these rocks? _____

_____

4. Draw six different-sized rocks. Label these rocks from **A** to **F**. Put them in order from smallest to largest by writing their letters on the blanks.

_____ smallest

_____

_____

_____

_____

_____ largest

Harcourt

Name _____

Date _____

Use Context to Determine/Confirm Word Meaning

Layers of Earth

Earth is made up of three different layers of rocks. The solid, outside layer of rock is called the <u>crust</u>. The middle layer of rock is called the <u>mantle</u>. The mantle is so hot that some of the rocks are nearly melted and are soft. The iron <u>core</u> is the center of Earth. Part of the core is solid and extremely hot. Another part of the core is hot liquid.

Look at the underlined terms. For each term, write word clues that help define the meaning of the term.

Term	Word Clues
crust	
mantle	
core	

Harcourt

Name _____

Date _____

What Are Minerals and Rocks?

Lesson Concept

A mineral is a solid natural material that has never been alive. Rocks are made of minerals.

Vocabulary

rock (C8) **core** (C8) **mantle** (C8) **crust** (C8) **mineral** (C6)

Match each term with its definition on the right.

1. rock

A hot middle layer of Earth

2. crust

B a solid substance made of minerals

3. mantle

C the center of Earth

4. core

D the solid outside layer of Earth

5. mineral

E a solid natural object that has never been alive

This drawing shows Earth cut open. Label each layer with a term from the vocabulary box.

6. _____

7. _____

8. _____

Harcourt

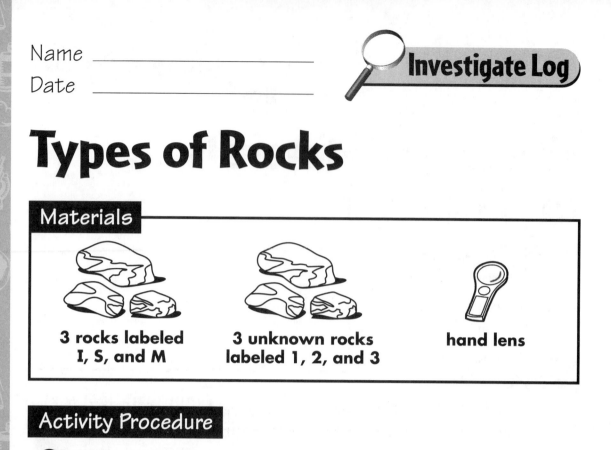
Types of Rocks

Materials

3 rocks labeled
I, S, and M

3 unknown rocks
labeled 1, 2, and 3

hand lens

Activity Procedure

1 Use the chart below.

2 Rocks *I*, *S*, and *M* are three different types of rocks. Look at them with and without the hand lens. **Record** your observations in the chart.

3 Look at each of the numbered rocks with and without the hand lens. **Record** your observations in the chart.

4 **Compare** the properties of the lettered rocks with the properties of the numbered rocks. Think about how the rocks are alike and how they are different.

Rock	Observations
I	
S	
M	
1	
2	
3	

Harcourt

Name _____

Draw Conclusions

1. What properties did you use to **compare** the rocks?

_____

_____

_____

2. Which numbered rock is most like Rock I? _____

Explain your answer. _____

_____

Which numbered rock is most like Rock S? _____

Explain your answer. _____

_____

Which numbered rock is most like Rock M? _____

Explain your answer. _____

_____

3. Scientists at Work Scientists learn about new objects when they **compare** them with objects they have already studied. What did you learn about the rocks when you compared them?

_____

_____

Investigate Further Look near your school or home for small rocks. **Compare** them with Rocks *I*, *S* and *M*. Try to **classify** the rocks as *I*, *S*, or *M*.

Harcourt

Name _____

Date _____

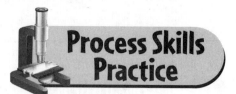

Compare and Observe

Think About Comparing and Observing

Diego's class went to a natural history museum to see an
exhibition of rocks. The next day his teacher gave them a
worksheet to fill out.

Rock 1   **Rock 2**   **Rock 3**   **Rock 4**

1. Look at the four rocks above. Name three properties of the rocks you

   can observe. _____

2. Which of the two rocks are similar? Rock _____ and Rock _____

3. Compare the two rocks. Which two properties are the same?

   _____

4. Compare Rock 1 and Rock 2. In what ways are they different from
   each other?

   _____

   _____

   _____

5. Why is it important to make good observations before you compare?

   _____

   _____

   _____

Harcourt

Arrange Events in Sequence

The sentences below are not in order. Rewrite the sentences in a paragraph that describes how some sedimentary rocks are formed.

Sediment then builds up in layers at the bottom of rivers, lakes, seas, and oceans.

Rivers carry sediment, or pieces of rocks and soil.

These layers are pressed and stuck together to form sedimentary rocks.

When a river slows down, it drops the sediment.

How Sedimentary Rocks Form

_____

_____

_____

_____

_____

_____

Rewrite this sentence to make it correct.

Igneous rock is rock that was once cooled and hardened but has melted.

_____

_____

Harcourt

How Do Rocks Form?

Lesson Concept

There are three types of rocks—igneous, sedimentary, and metamorphic.

Vocabulary

sedimentary rock (C12)	**igneous rock** (C12)
metamorphic rock (C12)	**rock cycle** (C14)

Write the letter of the best answer on the lines.

1. Rocks are grouped by how they _____.

   A melt   **B** change   **C** form

2. Rocks can be changed by heat and pressure, melting, and the effects of

_____.

   A wind and water   **B** cloud formations   **C** farming

3. After the material from an exploding volcano cools and hardens, _____ rocks can form.

   A metamorphic   **B** igneous   **C** sedimentary

4. Write about some of the ways you use rocks in the classroom.

_____

_____

5. Draw a sedimentary rock.

Harcourt

Name _____

Date _____

Investigate Log

Fossil Layers

Materials

5 colors of modeling clay

5 different seashells labeled A through E

5 sheets of wax paper

Activity Procedure

1 Use the chart below.

2 Use clay of one color to make a layer about the size and shape of a hamburger. Put the layer of clay on a sheet of wax paper.

3 Press a shell into the clay to make a print. Remove the shell. **Record** the clay color and the shell letter in your chart.

4 Place a sheet of wax paper over the clay layer.

5 Repeat Steps 2, 3, and 4 until you have made new layers with each color of clay and each shell.

Rock Layer	Clay Color	Shell Letter
1 (bottom layer)		
2		
3		
4		
5 (top layer)		

6 Trade your group's clay layers and
shells with another group's. Make a second chart. Remove each layer of
clay, and **observe** it. Do not change the order of the layers. Match each
shell to its print. Fill in the second chart. Check your answers with the
group that made the model.

Draw Conclusions

1. How did you know the correct layer for each shell?

_____

2. Pretend the shell prints are fossils and the clay is sedimentary rock. List
the shell letters from the oldest to the newest. Do this by using what you

know about sedimentary rock layers. _____

_____

_____

3. Scientists at Work Scientists **use models** to understand how things
happen. How did **using a model** help you understand how fossils are left

in layers in time order? _____

_____

_____

_____

Harcourt

Name _____

Date _____

Use a Model

Think About Using a Model

Shawna decided to make a model of a shell mold to help her understand how fossils are preserved. She mixed up some wet mud and half-filled a plastic margarine tub. She pressed a shell into the mud and covered it with more mud. She let the mud mixture dry in the sun for four days. Then she broke apart the mold, being careful not to disturb the mud below the shell.

1. Why might you use a model to find out about how fossils are preserved?

_____

_____

_____

2. What problems do you think there would be in recovering fossil prints from hardened mud?

_____

_____

3. What do you think Shawna saw after she broke open her mold?

_____

_____

4. Draw what you think Shawna saw.

Harcourt

Use Prefixes and Suffixes to Determine Word Meaning

What Fossils Are

Underline the prefix or suffix in each term. Then write the root word of each term. Use a dictionary to look up each term, and write its meaning in your own words.

1. fossil

    root word:

    definition of *fossilize:*

2.   print

    root word:

    definition of *imprint:*

3. predict

    root word:

    definition of *prediction:*

4. preserv

    root word:

    definition of *preservation:*

Harcourt

What Are Fossils?

Lesson Concept

A fossil is something that has lasted from a living thing that died long ago.

Vocabulary

fossil (C20)

Put a check mark in front of the true statement in each pair.

_____ **1.** Sedimentary rocks usually have more fossils than other rocks because heat and pressure help preserve the fossil.

_____ Sedimentary rocks usually have more fossils than other rocks because what's left of a plant or animal is trapped in the sediments that form the layers of the rock.

_____ **2.** Fossils can show the color of an animal that lived long ago.

_____ Fossils can show the shape of an animal that lived long ago.

_____ **3.** A mold is the shape of a plant or animal left in sediments when the rock formed.

_____ A mold is the imprint of a leaf or another thin object.

_____ **4.** A cast has the exact shape of the animal that made the mold.

_____ A cast always has a small piece of bone in the mold.

5. Explain how this mold formed.

_____

_____

_____

_____

Harcourt

Name _____

Date _____

Recognize Vocabulary

Fill in the blanks with the correct term from the box. Then find
the words and circle them in the word search puzzle.

mineral	rock	crust	mantle
core	fossil		

1. A solid object that was formed in nature and has never been alive is likely

to be a _____.

2. The surface layer of Earth is called the _____.

3. The _____ is the
middle layer of Earth.

4. At the center of Earth is the hottest layer

called the _____.

5. A _____ is made
of minerals.

6. A _____ is a thing
that has lasted from a living thing that
died long ago.

O	F	M	A	N	C	M
R	O	C	K	U	R	A
F	S	T	U	R	A	N
S	S	C	R	U	S	T
M	I	N	E	R	A	L
T	L	T	A	U	L	E
L	E	C	O	R	E	N

Read the sentences. Write the correct letter of the term on the lines.

A metamorphic rock	**B** sedimentary rock	**C** igneous rock

_____ **7.** It is a type of melted rock that has cooled and hardened.

_____ **8.** This rock forms from material that settles into layers.

_____ **9.** Heat and pressure have changed other rocks into this type of rock.

Harcourt

Name _____

Date _____

Write a "Rock" Song

Expressive Writing–Song Lyrics

Write lyrics for a song that describes the rock cycle. Use the idea web below to help you plan your song. Add information about how each type of rock is changed into the others.

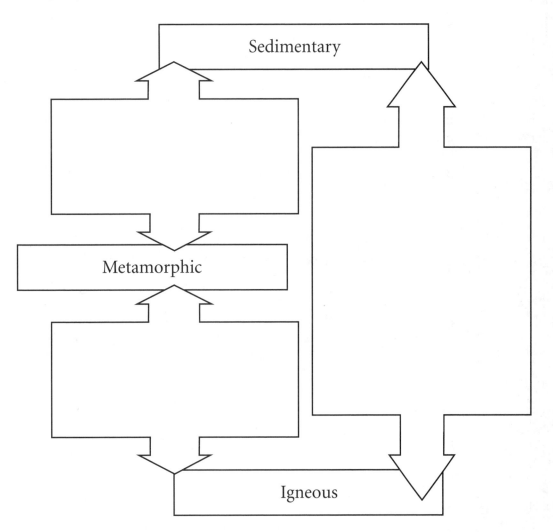

Harcourt

Name _____ Date _____

Forces That Shape the Land

Chapter 2 • Graphic Organizer for Chapter Concepts

LESSON 1
LANDFORMS

Types of Landforms

1. _____
2. _____
3. _____
4. _____
5. _____
6. _____

LESSON 2
SLOW LANDFORM CHANGES

Things That Weather Landforms

1. _____
2. _____
3. _____

Things That Erode
Weathered Rock

4. _____
5. _____
6. _____
7. _____

LESSON 3
RAPID LANDFORM CHANGES

Causes of Rapid Changes

1. _____
2. _____
3. _____

Name _____

Date _____

Folds in Earth's Crust

Materials

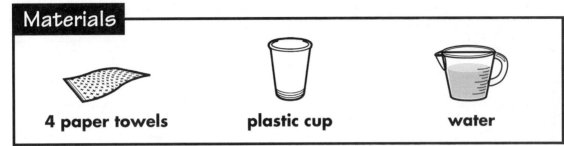

4 paper towels   plastic cup   water

Activity Procedure

1 Stack the four paper towels on a table. Fold the stack in half.

2 Sprinkle water on the towels. They should be damp but not very wet.

3 Place your hands on the edges of the damp towels.

4 Push the edges slowly toward the center.

Draw Conclusions

1. What happened as you pushed the edges of the towels together?

_____

_____

_____

2. How did the height of the towels change as you pushed them?

_____

_____

_____

Harcourt

3. Scientists at Work Scientists **use models** to understand how things happen. How did this model help you understand how mountains

form? _____

_____

_____

_____

Investigate Further Some mountains, such as the Rocky Mountains shown on page C33, form when two separate pieces of Earth's crust push together. How would you **make a model** to show this process?

My model: _____

_____

_____

_____

_____

_____

_____

Harcourt

Use a Model

Some things, like a flower blooming, take so long to happen, that they are hard to see. Other things, like a frog grabbing a fly with its tongue, happen so quickly that you don't see anything until it's over. You can learn more about something you can't easily see by using a model.

Think About Using a Model

Wong read that folds in Earth's surface can form mountains. The book said that it takes a lot of pressure to fold over the surface of Earth. He made a model so he could understand how much pressure. He took one sheet of newspaper and folded it in half. He continued to fold the newspaper in half as many times as he could. With each folding, the number of layers of paper doubled. After seven foldings, there were 128 layers. He observed that as the number of layers increased, he had to use more pressure to fold it.

1. What happened each time Wong folded the newspaper?

_____

_____

_____

2. How is Wong's model similar to folds in Earth's surface?

_____

_____

3. How did the model help Wong understand the amount of pressure

required to fold Earth's crust? _____

_____

_____

_____

Harcourt

Name _____

Date _____

Use Reference Sources

Earth's Surface

Use reference sources to gather information about the barrier islands in North Carolina called the Outer Banks. Write five fact cards, each telling one fact about the Outer Banks. At the bottom of the fact card, write your source. Cut out your fact cards, and compare them with other students' facts.

Facts About the Outer Banks in North Carolina

Reference Source: _____

Reference Source: _____

Reference Source: _____

Reference Source: _____

Reference Source: _____

Harcourt

Use with page C36.

Name _____

Date _____

Concept Review

What Are Landforms?

Lesson Concept

Landforms are the shapes, or features, found on Earth's surface.

Vocabulary

landform (C34)	**valley** (C35)	**plateau** (C35)
mountain (C35)	**plain** (C35)	**canyon** (C35)
barrier island (C35)		

Write the letter of the best answer on the lines.

1. A _____ is at least 600 meters higher than the land around it.

   A plateau   **B** tall hill   **C** mountain

2. When a river cuts a path through a plateau, a _____ can form.

   A canyon   **B** barrier island   **C** sand dune

3. Two flat areas on Earth's surface are _____.

   A valleys and   **B** plains and   **C** caverns and
       canyons   plateaus   mountains

Label each landform. Use the vocabulary list.

4. _____   **5.** _____   **6.** _____

Harcourt

Name _____

Date _____

Investigate Log

Sand at Work

Materials

sandstone rocks   sand   glass jar with lid

balance   extra masses for balance

Activity Procedure

1 Use the table below.

2 **Measure** the mass of all the rocks. **Record** your results in the table.

3 Fill the jar one-fourth full with sand. **Measure** the mass of the jar with the sand in it. **Record** your results. Add to get the total.

4 Put the rocks into the jar. Put the lid on. Shake the jar for 30 minutes. Then put the jar aside. Shake the jar for 30 minutes every day for one week.

5 After one week, **measure** the mass of the jar and its contents. Then remove the rocks from the jar. **Measure** their mass. **Record** your results. Subtract to find the mass of the jar with the sand inside.

	Mass of Rocks	Mass of Jar and Sand	Total Mass of Rocks, Jar, and Sand
Before			
After			

Harcourt

Name _____

Draw Conclusions

1. What did the sandstone look like before shaking?

_____

_____

Did it look different after shaking? How? _____

_____

_____

2. Compare the masses before and after the shaking. How did the mass of

the rocks change? _____

_____

3. Scientists at Work Scientists **interpret data** to understand how things
work. Use the data from this investigation to tell what happened to the
sand and the rock.

_____

_____

_____

Investigate further Design an experiment to test this **hypothesis:**
Larger pieces of rock weather faster.

Harcourt

Process Skills Practice

Interpreting Data

Data is information given to you or information you gather during activities. When you interpret data, you decide what it means.

Think About Interpreting Data

Andrea gathered data on the wearing away of rocks. She worked with a piece of siltstone and a piece of limestone. Before beginning, she measured each of the rocks and recorded her data. She rubbed a small file back and forth over each rock. The file acted like grains of sand blown by the wind against the rocks. Siltstone is a soft rock, so many pieces fell off as Andrea rubbed the file back and forth. Limestone is a harder rock. Only a few pieces fell off.

	Siltstone	**Limestone**
Size at the beginning	6 centimeters	6 centimeters
Size at the end	2 centimeters	5 centimeters
Amount of stone that wore off	4 centimeters	1 centimeter

1. Which stone was larger at the end of the experiment? _____

2. Which stone was smaller at the end of the experiment?

_____

3. What do you think the surface of the siltstone would look like after it had

been rubbed with the file? _____

_____

4. What is the reason so much more of the siltstone wore off than the

limestone? _____

5. How is rubbing a file on the rock like wind wearing away rock?

_____

_____

Harcourt

Use with page C39.

Name _____

Date _____

Summarize and Paraphrase a Selection

Changes to Land

Read the paragraph. Then make an outline about Sleeping Bear Dunes.

Sleeping Bear Dunes

A dune is formed when wind blows sand into a large mound. One of the world's largest areas of dunes, called Sleeping Bear Dunes, is found in the northwestern part of Michigan's Lower Peninsula. The dunes run along the shore of Lake Michigan and stretch over 11 kilometers (7 mi). The dunes rise about 152 meters (500 ft) above the lake. Beach grass and sand cherry are plants that grow in the dunes. Animals that live in and around the dunes include bobcats, deer, skunks, and porcupines. Sleeping Bear Dunes was named after a Chippewa Indian legend.

I.

  A. _____

     1. _____

     2. _____

     3. _____

     4. _____

        _____

     5. _____

        _____

Harcourt

Use with pages C42–C43.

What Are Slow Landform Changes?

Lesson Concept

Wind, water, gravity, and glaciers slowly shape the land by weathering and eroding rock and soil.

Vocabulary

weathering (C40)   **erosion** (C42)   **glacier** (C44)

The following sentences about weathering and erosion are mixed up. Number them in order from 1 to 3.

_____ **1.** Erosion moves the broken rocks around.

_____ **2.** Water flows into the holes and cracks in one of the broken rocks. The water freezes. The force of the ice breaks the rock into more pieces.

_____ **3.** The wind blows hard. It blows against rocks and wears them down. The rocks break apart.

4. Which of these things can break rocks? Circle the letter of your answer.

A wind   **B** water   **C** ice   **D** plants   **E** all of them

5. When Jack was in kindergarten, he saw a fence on the edge of a hill. After a few years, he saw that the fence had moved a few inches down the hill. Creep caused the fence to move. Explain the process of creep.

_____

_____

Harcourt

A Model Volcano

Materials

safety goggles **soil** **flour** **water**

large tray **baking soda** **wax paper** **lab apron** **measuring spoons**

red, green, and blue food coloring **tall, thin, plastic jar** **measuring cup** **white vinegar**

 CAUTION

Activity Procedure

1 Cover the tray with wax paper. Place the jar in the middle of the tray.

2 **CAUTION** **Put on safety goggles and a lab apron.** Mix $\frac{1}{2}$ teaspoon flour and 1 teaspoon baking soda in a measuring cup. Put this mixture into the jar. Add 10 drops of red food coloring.

3 Moisten the soil slightly. Put the soil around the jar. Then mold the soil into the shape of a volcano. The top of the jar must be even with the top of the soil.

4 Slowly pour $\frac{1}{4}$ cup white vinegar into the jar.

5 **Observe** what happens. Remove the jar and throw away the contents. Replace the jar. Then wait 15 minutes for the "lava" to dry.

Harcourt

Investigate Log

6 Repeat Steps 2, 4, and 5 with the
green food coloring and then with the blue food coloring.

Draw Conclusions

1. What happened when you poured the vinegar into the mixture in the jar?

_____

_____

2. What did the material that came out of your volcano stand for?

_____

3. Scientists at Work Scientists **make a model** to understand how things
happen in nature that are difficult to **observe** in person. How did your
model help you understand the way an erupting volcano changes the

land around it? _____

_____

_____

_____

Investigate Further Different kinds of volcanoes have different kinds of
eruptions. How could you find out what these eruptions are like? Choose
one type of eruption, and **plan and conduct an investigation** to model it.

Type of eruption: _____

Investigation plan: _____

_____

_____

My observations: _____

_____

_____

How this eruption works: _____

_____

_____

Harcourt

Make a Model

Sometimes you can't observe things because they could hurt you. Other times you can't observe things because you can't get to them. You can make a model to help you understand things in nature that you can't observe in person.

Think About Making a Model

A shield volcano is one kind of volcanic landform. Shield volcanoes have gentle slopes. The lava from shield volcanoes is hot and takes a long time to cool down to become a solid. So when a shield volcano erupts, the lava travels far from the vent. Jonathan knew he couldn't watch an actual shield volcano erupt. He decided to make a model instead.

First he taped a film canister to the center of a piece of cardboard. Next he used clay to shape a mountain around the film canister. He made sure to leave a hole at the top for the lava to come through. When he finished making the mountain, he put in the film canister liquid that erupted like lava.

1. How did Jonathan shape his mountain to make it like a shield volcano?

_____

_____

2. What did the lava in the model have to do to be like the lava of a shield

volcano? _____

_____

Harcourt

Name _____

Date _____

Use Context to Determine/Confirm Word Meaning

Rapid Changes to the Land

Read the sentences. Look at the underlined words. In the spaces below each sentence, write the clue word or words that might help you know the meaning of the underlined term.

1. The San Andreas <u>fault</u> is a crack in Earth's crust in California.

_____

2. Some earthquakes can cause big sea waves called <u>tsunamis</u>, which can flood coasts.

_____

3. A volcanic <u>eruption</u> can send out hot clouds of ash, rock, and gases.

_____

4. Some volcanic eruptions spill thick, hot <u>lava</u> down the sides of the volcano.

_____

5. If a river can't hold all the rainwater that runs into it, it may overflow its banks and <u>flood</u>.

_____

Harcourt

Name _____

Date _____

What Are Rapid Landform Changes?

Lesson Concept

Earthquakes, volcanoes, and floods can change Earth's surface quickly.

Vocabulary

earthquake (C48)	**volcano** (C49)	**flood** (C50)

Use the vocabulary words above to fill in the blanks.

1. _____ can wash away soil and buildings, but leave a new layer of soil on the land.

2. Buildings can be destroyed when an _____ shakes Earth's surface.

3. _____ spread lava, ash, or mud in large areas around them.

The following sentences about flooding are mixed up. Number them in the right order from 1 to 5.

_____ **4.** Rainwater runs into a river.

_____ **5.** A storm dumps heavy rain on the land.

_____ **6.** The flood water flows into a farm near the river.

_____ **7.** The river cannot hold all the water.

_____ **8.** The river overflows its banks and causes a flood.

Harcourt

Name _____

Date _____

Recognize Vocabulary

Match the terms at the right with the definitions on the left.

landform	mountain	valley	canyon
plain	plateau	flood	weathering
erosion	glacier	volcano	earthquake
barrier island			

_____ **1.** the way rocks are broken down into smaller pieces

_____ **2.** movement of weathered rock

_____ **3.** huge sheet of ice that slowly moves downhill

_____ **4.** shaking of Earth's surface by moving of the crust or mantle

_____ **5.** opening in Earth's surface from which lava flows

_____ **6.** large amount of water that covers normally dry land

_____ **7.** shape or feature on Earth's surface

_____ **8.** a place on Earth's surface that is much higher than the land around it

_____ **9.** a lowland area between higher lands, such as mountains

_____ **10.** a deep valley with very steep sides

_____ **11.** a flat area on Earth's surface

_____ **12.** a flat area higher than the land around it

_____ **13.** a thin island near a coast

A mountain

B volcano

C plateau

D barrier island

E weathering

F earthquake

G plain

H erosion

I landform

J glacier

K flood

L valley

M canyon

Use with pages C32–C51.

Write an Editorial

Persuasive Writing–Opinion

Imagine that you are the editor of a science magazine. You have heard that the government will pay for scientists to study one land-changing force. The money should go to the study that helps prevent the worst disasters. Write an editorial telling whether the scientists should use the money to study earthquakes, volcanoes, or floods. Support your opinion with details. Use the organizer below to plan your editorial.

State your opinion.
State reasons.   **Reason 1:**
Reason 2:
Reason 3:
Restate your opinion or call for action.

Name _____ Date _____

Soils

LESSON 1
HOW SOILS FORM

Parts of Soil

1. _____

2. _____

3. _____

4. _____

LESSON 2
HOW SOILS DIFFER

What Makes Soils Different

1. _____

2. _____

3. _____

LESSON 3
CONSERVING SOILS

How Soils Can Be Harmed

1. _____

2. _____

How Soils Can Be Saved

3. _____

4. _____

Harcourt

Name _____

Date _____

Enrich the Soil

Materials

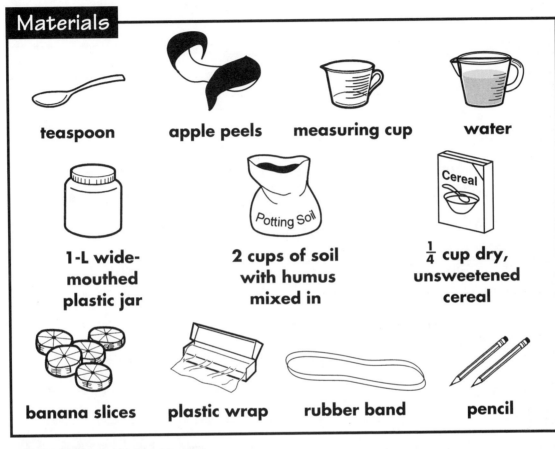

teaspoon

apple peels

measuring cup

water

1-L wide-mouthed plastic jar

2 cups of soil with humus mixed in

$\frac{1}{4}$ cup dry, unsweetened cereal

banana slices

plastic wrap

rubber band

pencil

Activity Procedure

1 Put one cup of soil into the jar. Sprinkle two teaspoons of water on top of the soil.

2 Spread the fruit and cereal on top of the soil. The apple peels and banana slices must touch the sides of the jar.

3 Put another cup of soil on top of the fruit and cereal. You should see pieces of fruit and cereal through the sides of the jar.

4 Cover the jar with plastic wrap. Put a rubber band around the jar to hold the plastic wrap. Use a pencil point to make three small holes in the plastic wrap.

5 Leave the jar in a warm place, but do not put it in direct sunlight. Keep the jar there for four weeks.

6 Look at the jar once each week for four weeks. **Record** what you **observe**.

Use with pages C60–C61.   (page 1 of 2)

Name _____

Draw Conclusions

1. What changes did you **observe** in the jar after one week?

_____

_____

After four weeks? _____

_____

_____

2. **Form a hypothesis** about what would happen to the soil after eight weeks. To form your hypothesis, finish this sentence: After eight weeks, the soil will. . . . _____

_____

_____

Explain. _____

_____

_____

_____

3. **Scientists at Work** Scientists use their observations to form hypotheses. How did you use observations to form your hypothesis?

_____

_____

_____

Investigate Further **Form a hypothesis** about the effects of compost on plant growth. **Plan an experiment** to test your hypothesis.

Plan: _____

_____

Results: _____

_____

Harcourt

Name _____

Date _____

Hypothesize

Hypothesizing is making a statement about what you think will happen. To make a hypothesis, you use your observations.

Think About Predicting

Plants take in the nutrients they need from the soil in which they grow. Compost is a mixture of rotten plant and animal matter. It is dark-colored and has lots of nutrients in it. Plain soil is light in color and contains few nutrients. Soil becomes darker in color and richer in nutrients as compost is added to it.

Martina's science teacher asked her to grow a cucumber plant. Martina knows cucumber plants need lots of nutrients. Look at the jars of soil below. Help Martina decide which soil to use for her cucumber plant.

1. What do you hypothesize will happen to a cucumber plant in Jar 1?

   Explain. _____

   _____

2. What do you hypothesize will happen to a cucumber plant in Jar 2?

   Explain. _____

   _____

   _____

3. Which soil should Martina use? Explain. _____

   _____

   _____

Use with page C61.

Name _____

Date _____

Summarize and Paraphrase a Selection

Earthworms

Earthworms make their homes in soil. They need dark, wet places to live. As they make tunnels, worms use the soil for food. When earthworms take particles of soil into their mouths, they don't use all the soil for food. Once the soil is in their bodies, organic material such as bits of plants are used for food. Other materials, such as rock, are passed through each earthworm's body. The waste is then deposited back into the soil.

Earthworms are different sizes and colors. Most earthworms are small, growing to 25 centimeters (10 in.) long. One kind of earthworm from Australia can grow to 3.3 meters (about 11 ft) long! The most common earthworm is reddish-brown. Some earthworms from Britain are green.

1. What are the two main ideas of the selection?

_____

_____

2. Write a summary of the selection. Be sure to include information that supports the main ideas of your summary.

_____

_____

_____

_____

Harcourt

Name _____

Date _____

 **Concept Review**

How Do Soils Form?

Soil is important to all living things. It takes a long time to form, so we must take care of it.

Vocabulary

soil (C62)   **humus** (C62)   **bedrock** (C63)   **topsoil** (C63)

Write the letter of the best answer on the lines.

1. Soil is a mixture of _____ parts.

   A six   **B** three   **C** four

2. Deep soil takes _____ to form.

   A 50 years   **B** 500 to 1,000 years   **C** thousands of years

3. Humus is made up of decayed parts of _____.

   A rocks   **B** once living things   **C** fossils

4. Soil contains the _____ that all living things need for growth.

   A minerals   **B** vegetables   **C** compost

Look at the picture. Label these parts of the soil: topsoil, subsoil, and bedrock.

_____

_____

_____

Harcourt

Investigate Log

Types of Soil

Materials

2 soil samples

low-power microscope

toothpick

paper plates

petri dish

paper towel

Activity Procedure

1 Get two soil samples from your teacher.

2 Place a few grains of one sample in the petri dish. Put the dish under the microscope.

3 **Observe** the soil. Move the soil grains around with the toothpick. What do the grains look like? **Record** what you **observe**. Make a drawing of the grains.

My observations: _____

_____

4 Pick up some soil from the petri dish. Rub it between your fingers. How does it feel? **Record** what you **observe**.

My observations: _____

_____

5 Clean the petri dish with the paper towel. Repeat Steps 2 through 4 with the other soil sample.

Harcourt

Name _____

Investigate Log

Draw Conclusions

1. What senses did you use to **observe** the soil? _____

_____

2. Describe your observations. _____

_____

_____

_____

3. Scientists at Work Scientists **observe** to see how things are alike and how they are different. How were the soil samples alike? How were

they different? _____

_____

_____

_____

_____

_____

Investigate Further Experiment to find another way soils differ. How much water can different soils hold? Get two different types of soil from your teacher. Put each type into a separate jar. Now get two cups of water from your teacher. Pour one of the cups of water into each jar of soil.

Which soil holds more water? _____

_____

_____

How do you know? _____

_____

_____

_____

Harcourt

Name _____

Date _____

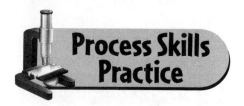

Observe

Sometimes you can tell a lot about something by using only one of
your senses to observe it. Sometimes you can't. You may need to
use more than one sense to observe something.

Think About Observing

Brandon needs to choose soil for a houseplant. He doesn't know whether to
use soil from his backyard or potting soil. The soil from the backyard is light
colored and has a lot of sand in it. The potting soil looks dark and has very
little sand.

Brandon puts backyard soil in one plant pot and potting soil in another.
Each pot has a hole in the bottom to drain water. He pours a cup of water
into each pot of soil. Most of the water comes out of the pot with the
backyard soil. Very little water comes out of the pot containing potting soil.

Backyard Soil   **Potting Soil**

1. What observations did Brandon make about the samples from looking at

   them? _____

   _____

2. What observations could he have made with some of his other senses?

   _____

   _____

3. If his plant needs a lot of water, which soil should he use? Explain.

   _____

   _____

   _____

Harcourt

Name _____

Date _____

Use Context to Determine/Confirm Word Meaning

Soils and Growing Plants

Use the sentences before and after the underlined terms to write their definitions. Then use a dictionary to look up each term. Complete the chart and compare your definitions.

Some soils are very good for growing plants. Topsoil is a type of soil that is good for growing plants. It is the top layer of the soil and contains the most humus. Humus contains much of what plants need for growth. Humus is the part of the soil made of decayed parts of once-living things. Good topsoils have the right mixture of minerals and humus. Some soils can be changed to make them better for growing plants. Farmers can add fertilizers to poor soils. Fertilizers are materials that are rich in the things plants need for growth.

Your Definition Using Context Clues	Dictionary Definition
topsoil:	topsoil:
humus:	humus:
fertilizers:	fertilizers:

Harcourt

Use with page C70.

How Do Soils Differ?

Lesson Concept

There are many types of soils. They have different colors and different-sized grains. They also have different mixtures of minerals and humus.

Vocabulary

clay (C69)	loam (C70)

Answer the following questions about soil.

1. Your family fills the backyard sandbox with fresh sand. There is some sand left over. Would it be a good idea to use the sand for planting bean

plants? Why or why not? _____

_____

2. Circle each of the elements that help make topsoil good for growing plants.

   A a good mixture of minerals and humus   **B** good drainage

   C a high percentage of wet clay   **D** plenty of water and air

3. Put a check mark next to the statements that are correct.

   _____ All soils feel the same.   _____ Sandy soil feels gritty.

   _____ Some kinds of soil do not hold water.

Underline the best answer.

4. This is rich topsoil with lots of humus, water, and air for plants.

   A clay   **B** loam

5. This soil is made of small grains and feels like powder when it is dry.

   A clay   **B** loam

Harcourt

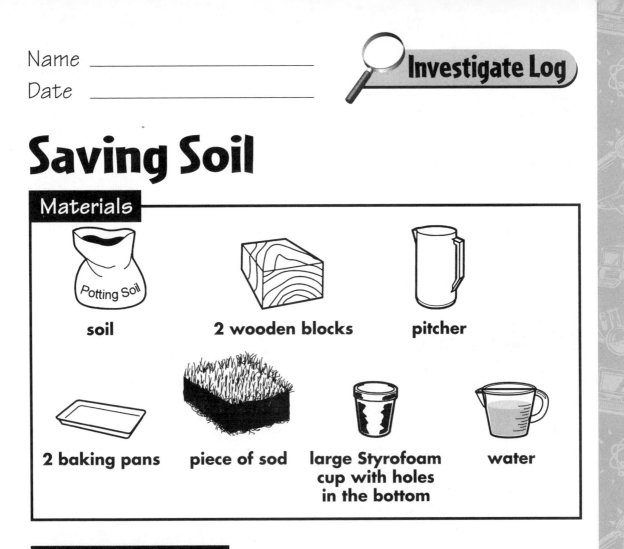

🔍 **Investigate Log**

Saving Soil

Materials

soil   2 wooden blocks   pitcher

2 baking pans   piece of sod   large Styrofoam cup with holes in the bottom   water

Activity Procedure

1 Put soil in both baking pans. Put sod over the soil in one pan.

2 Set one end of each pan on a wooden block. One end of each pan should be lower than the other.

3 **Predict** what will happen when water is dripped into each pan. **Record** your prediction.

My prediction: _____

_____

4 **Make a model** of rain over the pan that has just soil. Have one person hold the cup over the upper end of the pan. Have another person pour water from the pitcher into the cup.

5 **Observe** what happens in the pan. **Record** what you see.

_____

Harcourt

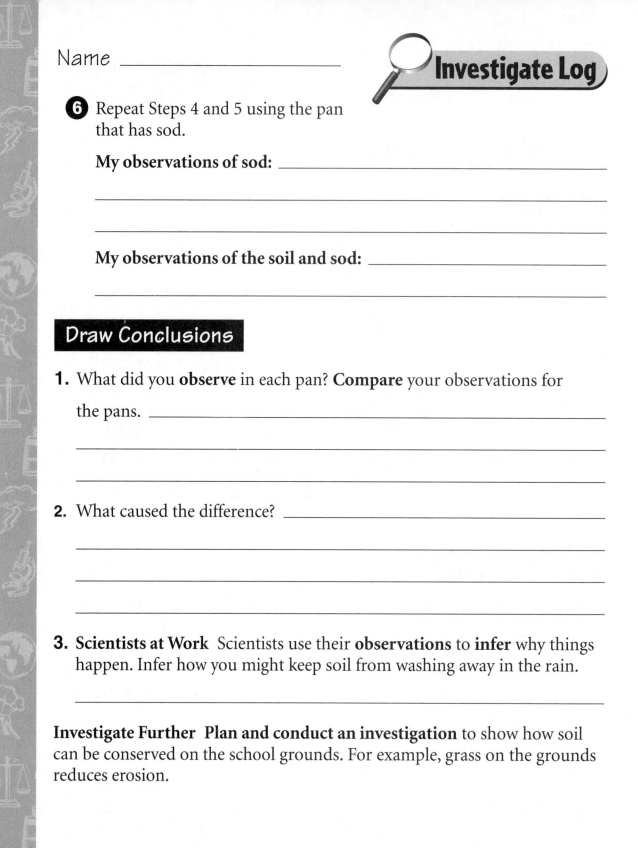

Investigate Log

6 Repeat Steps 4 and 5 using the pan that has sod.

My observations of sod: _____

_____

_____

My observations of the soil and sod: _____

_____

Draw Conclusions

1. What did you **observe** in each pan? **Compare** your observations for the pans. _____

_____

_____

2. What caused the difference? _____

_____

_____

_____

3. Scientists at Work Scientists use their **observations** to **infer** why things happen. Infer how you might keep soil from washing away in the rain.

_____

Investigate Further Plan and conduct an investigation to show how soil can be conserved on the school grounds. For example, grass on the grounds reduces erosion.

Harcourt

Name _____

Date _____

Observe and Infer

When you observe something, you use your senses to study what happens. Inferring is using what you have observed to explain what has happened.

Think About Observing and Inferring

Alicia and Mary wanted to find out how rain erodes bare soil. They dug up two piles of soil about half a meter high. They shaped the piles of soil into mounds. They put a metric ruler into each mound so that only the top 5 centimeters were visible. They put a sheet of newspaper over one of the mounds. Using a watering can, they sprinkled 2 liters of water over each mound. They observed the rulers and noted that the ruler in the uncovered mound showed more centimeter lines than the other.

Before Watering   **After Watering**

1. Describe the mounds before they were watered. _____

_____

_____

_____

2. Describe the mounds after they were watered. _____

_____

_____

3. What inference can you make about bare ground and rain?

_____

_____

Harcourt

Name _____

Date _____

Reading Skills Practice

Use Prefixes and Suffixes to Determine Word Meaning

The -ation and -ing Suffixes

The -*ation* and -*ing* suffixes change an action word (verb) into a word that names the action (noun).

Example

Action word (verb):	conserve
Definition:	to save resources by using them carefully
Suffix:	-ation
New action word (noun):	conservation
Definition:	the act of conserving

Use a dictionary and the sample above to help you complete the information for the terms below.

1. Action word (verb): ___restore_____

Definition: _____

_____

Suffix: ___-ation_____

New action word (noun): _____

Definition: _____

2. Action word (verb): ___till_____

Definition: _____

Suffix: ___-ing_____

New action word (noun): _____

Definition: _____

Harcourt

Name _____

Date _____

How Can We Conserve Soil?

Lesson Concept

Soil that is overused or exposed can erode. Farmers conserve soil by strip cropping, contour plowing, and other methods.

Vocabulary

conservation (C76)	**resource** (C74)
contour plowing (C76)	**strip cropping** (C76)

Write the letter of the best answer on the lines.

1. Soil is important because it is one of Earth's most important _____.

   A products   **B** resources   **C** minerals

2. One way to conserve soil is to plant _____ types of crops each year.

   A different   **B** the same   **C** water saving

3. Contour plowing is _____.

   A planting thick mats of plants between crops

   B planting low-lying plants that barely cover the ground

   C planting crops around the sides of hills

4. Strip cropping is _____.

   A planting strips of thick grass or clover between strips of crops

   B stripping crops when they are ripe

   C putting in dead plant material between plant rows

What can happen to tilled soil during the winter? _____

_____

Harcourt

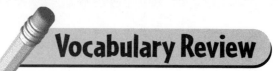

Vocabulary Review

Recognize Vocabulary

soil	humus	topsoil
clay	loam	resource
conservation	strip cropping	contour plowing
bedrock		

Read the sentences. Unscramble the scrambled words, and write them on the lines.

1. **Lios** is the loose material in which plants can grow in the upper layer of Earth. _____

2. **Shumu** is the part of soil made up of decayed parts of once-living things. _____

3. **Pitools** is the top layer of soil. _____

4. **Lyca** soil has small grains and small spaces between the grains. _____

5. **Maol** is a rich soil with lots of humus. _____

6. A **croesuer** is a material found in nature that living things use. _____

7. Saving resources by using them carefully is called **scanernotiov**. _____

8. Planting strips of grass between crops is called **ripst grocpinp**. _____

9. Planting crops around a hillside instead of up and down is **toucorn wingolp**. _____

10. **Kcordeb** is the solid rock that is underneath the soil. _____

Harcourt

Name _____

Date _____

Writing Practice

Write a Letter About Soil

Expressive Writing—Friendly Letter

Write a letter to a friend or family member who lives in another part of the country. In your letter, tell what you are learning about soil. Describe the soil where you live. Ask your friend or family member to write back with a description of the soil where he or she lives. Use the letter format below to help you plan your letter.

Heading
Your address:

Today's date:

Greeting
Dear _____ ,

Body of Letter

First Paragraph:

Second Paragraph:

Closing

Your friend,

_____

Use with pages C82–C83.

Harcourt

Name _____ Date _____

Earth's Resources

WHAT ARE RESOURCES?

Where Resources Are Found

_____ Earth's surface

Example: _____

_____ Earth's surface

Example: _____

_____ Earth's surface

Example: _____

How Resources Are Removed
From Earth's Crust

_____

_____

DIFFERENT KINDS OF RESOURCES

Renewable Resources

Example: _____

Two ways these resources are used

_____

Reusable Resources

Examples: _____

Two ways these resources are used

_____

Nonrenewable Resources

Examples: _____

Two ways these resources are used

_____

CONSERVING RESOURCES

Things That Can Be Recycled

_____

_____

How Resources That Aren't
Recycled Can Be Saved

_____

_____

How You Can Help Reduce
Pollution

_____

_____

_____

Harcourt

Mining Resources

Materials

oatmeal-raisin cookie

dropper

toothpick

paper plate

water

Activity Procedure

1 **Observe** your cookie. How many raisins do you see? _____

2 Fill the dropper with water. Put a few drops of water around each raisin. The cookie should be moist but not wet.

3 Use the toothpick to "mine" all the raisins from the cookie. If the raisins are hard to get out, put a few more drops of water around them. Put the removed raisins on the plate.

4 **Observe** the cookie again. Were there any raisins you didn't see in the cookie the first time? Why didn't you see them?

_____

_____

_____

Harcourt

Name _____

Draw Conclusions

1. What did you "mine" from the cookie? _____

2. How did the water help you? _____
_____
_____

3. How is mining raisins from a cookie like mining materials from the
   Earth? _____
_____
_____
_____
_____

4. **Scientists at Work** Scientists **observe** things to see how they work.
   They use their observations to **infer** how similar things work. Use your
   observations to infer how mining could affect the land around the mine.
_____
_____
_____
_____
_____
_____
_____

Harcourt

Name _____

Date _____

Observe and Infer

Using your senses helps you observe. You can note what happens in your observations. You then infer by using your observations to form an idea of how things work.

Think About Observing and Inferring

Hydraulic (hy•DRAW•lik) mining is a form of gold mining used in the 1800s. Miners used huge hoses that sprayed water on a cliff. The water washed away chunks of rock. This process ruined the land.

   Some students set up an experiment to model hydraulic mining. They buried a number of pebbles in a hill of soil. The pebbles were the models of gold. The students sprayed water on the hill with a garden hose. The water washed away the soil. The pebbles rolled out of the hill.

1. What did these students observe before the hill was sprayed and after it

   was sprayed? _____

   _____

   _____

   _____

2. What was being "mined" in the experiment? _____

3. How did the water help remove the pebbles from the hill?

   _____

4. What inference can you make about why this is bad for the land?

   _____

Harcourt

Name _____

Date _____

Summarize and Paraphrase a Selection

Oil Is a Resource Important to Your Home

Many resources are important to everyday life in the home. Oil is one important resource that is pumped from Earth's crust.

People use oil for many things. Plastic is made from some of the things found in oil. Plastic is used to make many things, such as food containers, toys, and even the parts of vacuum cleaners.

Gasoline is a fuel that comes from oil. Most cars and trucks use gasoline. Some lawn mowers and weed trimmers use gasoline and oil.

Some homes use oil as fuel for heating. Some power plants burn oil to produce electricity. Electricity is an important power source for most homes. Electricity is used for lights, heat, air conditioning, and appliances.

Oil is a resource that is very important to many people.

Write a summary of the selection. Use your own words.

_____

_____

_____

_____

_____

_____

_____

_____

_____

_____

Use with page C89.

Name _____

Date _____

What Are Resources?

A resource is a material that living things use. We use resources to live and make things we need.

resource (C88)

1. Circle each resource that is found under Earth's surface.

   A oil   **B** air   **C** coal   **D** diamonds

2. Circle each item that is a resource.

   A air   **B** animals   **C** water   **D** soil

3. Circle each resource that is found on Earth's surface.

   A soil   **B** air   **C** water   **D** oil

4. What are three ways resources are brought up from under Earth's surface?

_____

_____

_____

List as many resources as you can that you use during one day.

_____   _____   _____

_____   _____   _____

_____   _____   _____

_____   _____   _____

_____   _____   _____

Use with page C91.

Name _____

Date _____

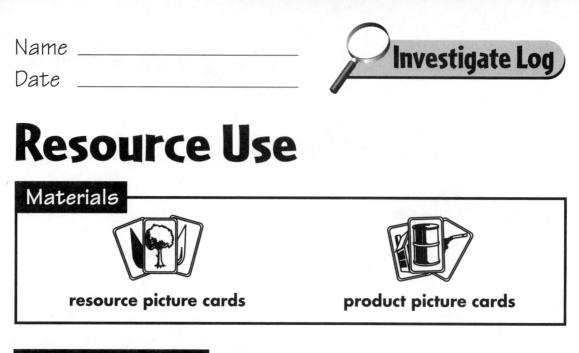

Resource Use

Materials

resource picture cards

product picture cards

Activity Procedure

1 Look closely at all the cards. Sort the cards into two groups—resources and products.

2 **Classify** the products. To do this, match each product with the resource from which it comes.

3 Make a drawing to show how you sorted your cards.

Harcourt

Name _____

Draw Conclusions

1. How did you **classify** the products? _____

_____

_____

_____

2. Does a product always look like the resource it was made from? Explain.

_____

_____

_____

3. Scientists at Work Scientists **compare** objects to see how they are alike and how they are different. How did comparing the products to the

resources help you **classify** the products? _____

_____

Investigate Further Identify five or more products in your home. **Classify** the products by the resources they came from.

	Products	Resources
1		
2		
3		
4		
5		
6		
7		

Harcourt

Name _____

Date _____

Compare and Classify

When you compare things, you think about how they are alike and how they are different. Classifying is a way to put objects that are alike into groups.

Think About Comparing and Classifying

The pictures below show three products and three resources from which the products come. Compare the items you see. Identify the products and the resources. Use the chart to list your classifications.

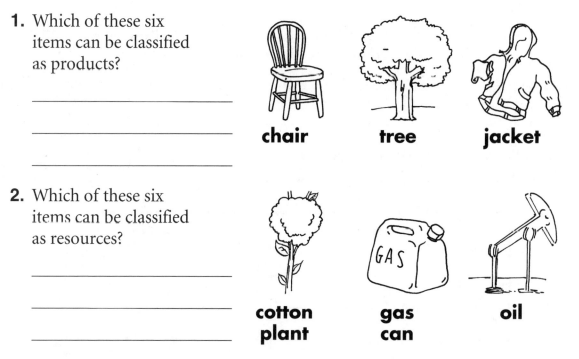

1. Which of these six items can be classified as products?

   _____

   _____

   _____

   chair   **tree**   **jacket**

2. Which of these six items can be classified as resources?

   _____

   _____

   _____

   cotton plant   **gas can**   **oil**

3. Another way to classify these items is to match each product with the resource from which it comes. Do this by filling in the chart below.

Product			
Resource from Which It Comes			

Harcourt

Identify Cause and Effect

Renewable and Nonrenewable Resources

A nonrenewable resource will not last forever. Copper, oil, and iron are examples of nonrenewable resources.

Read the selections below, looking for causes and effects. Underline the cause and circle the effect in each selection.

1. Wood is used for building, and paper comes from trees. When trees are replanted, this resource is renewed for the future.

2. The sun never stops shining. When the sun shines on Earth, living things use the sun's energy to meet their needs.

3. People use water for cooking and bathing. Once this water has been dirtied, it must be cleaned before it can be used again.

4. Some kinds of old growth forests are cut down. It will take hundreds of years for another old growth forest to grow.

5. The United States mines a lot of coal. When all the coal has been burned, another fuel will have to be used.

6. People use natural gas to heat homes and cook food. When all the natural gas has been burned, there will be no more for people to use.

Harcourt

What Are the Different Kinds of Resources?

Lesson Concept

Resources can be renewable, reusable, or nonrenewable.

Vocabulary

renewable resource (C94)   **reusable resource** (C94)

nonrenewable resource (C96)

Make a check mark in front of the statements that are true.

_____ **1.** An old growth forest is a reusable resource.

_____ **2.** Soil is a nonrenewable resource.

_____ **3.** Water and air are reusable resources.

4. Draw a picture of a reusable resource. Explain why the resource is reusable.

5. Name one nonrenewable resource you care about. Give some ideas for

caring for that resource. _____

_____

_____

Harcourt

Name _____

Date _____

 Investigate Log

Recycling

Materials

aluminum cans your
family uses in one week

large plastic
trash bag

bathroom
scale

Activity Procedure

1 Get permission from a parent to participate in this activity. Save all of the aluminum cans your family uses for one week. Rinse them in the sink. Put the cans in the trash bag.

2 Weigh the cans. If your cans are too light to weigh, you can find their weight by multiplying the number of cans you have collected by 1.5 oz. **Record** the weight.

3 Bring your results to class. Use your data to draw a bar on the class graph. The graph will show the weight of each family's cans.

4 Add up all the weights shown on the graph. The sum tells you how much aluminum all the families used in one week.

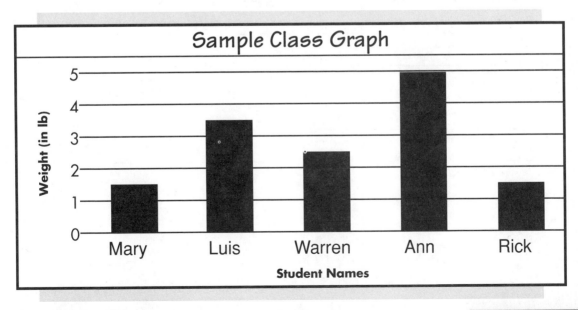

Sample Class Graph — Weight (in lb) vs. Student Names (Mary, Luis, Warren, Ann, Rick)

Draw Conclusions

1. Suppose that 1 lb of cans takes up 2 ft of space. How much landfill space would your class save by recycling all the cans you saved this week?

_____

_____

_____

_____

_____

_____

2. What other resources might be saved if your cans were recycled instead of thrown away? _____

_____

_____

_____

_____

3. **Scientists at Work** There are many ways you could tell someone how much aluminum was used in one week. In this investigation you **used numbers** to describe the weight of aluminum used. How does using numbers help you tell people what you found out?

_____

_____

_____

_____

_____

Harcourt

Name _____

Date _____

Use Numbers

Using numbers gives you exact amounts of things. You can use numbers to tell others about data you've collected.

Think About Using Numbers

Savannah goes to a recycling center. People drive up and unload their recyclables. Trucks come in filled with newspapers, glass bottles and jars, soda cans, and aluminum food cans. A large sign lists the number and weight of the objects that come in each half-hour. Savannah wants to report back to her class what she sees. She makes a chart. She records the weight of the paper and the number of items recycled while she was there.

Glass	Aluminum	Paper
300 bottles	500 soda cans	1,814 kg
150 jars	250 food cans	

1. List the total number of glass items recorded on the chart. _____

2. List the total number of aluminum cans recorded on the chart. _____

3. A sign at the center says "For every 907 kilograms (2,000 lb) of paper recycled, 17 trees are saved." If the sign is correct, how many trees are saved by recycling 1,814 kilograms of paper? _____

4. How did using numbers help Savannah tell people what she found out?

_____

_____

_____

Harcourt

Name _____

Date _____

Use Prefixes and Suffixes to Determine Word Meaning

In the chart below, identify the prefix or suffix in each word. Then identify the root word. Tell how the word with the prefix or suffix is different from the root word. You may use a dictionary to help you.

Conserving Resources

Term	Root Word	Prefix or Suffix	How is the term different from its root word?
reuse			
healthful			
unhealthful			
nonrenewable			

Use with page C102.

Name _____

Date _____

How Can We Conserve Earth's Resources?

Lesson Concept

We can conserve resources by using fewer resources or by recycling.

Vocabulary

recycle (C100)

Circle the best answer in each sentence.

1. Tuesday is trash pickup day in Jason's neighborhood. Trash is picked up and taken to the   **recycling center • landfill**   where it is buried in the ground.

2. Jason and his classmates started a   **fuel oil • recyclable**   collection program in their classroom. They made containers for aluminum cans and glass bottles. They set up some boxes for used paper. The program helped save energy and reduce pollution.

3. Jason decided to find out where the aluminum for their soft drink cans comes from. He learned that aluminum comes from **bauxite • ammonite** ore. The ore is mined. He also learned that aluminum is a nonrenewable resource.

4. Jason's class learned that some resources cannot be recycled, but they can be   **conserved • renewed**   in a number of ways. Jason decided to turn off lights when he wasn't using them. He decided to walk or ride his bike whenever possible.

5. What are your ideas for recycling and using fewer resources?

_____

_____

Harcourt

Recognize Vocabulary

Choose the best term to complete the sentences. Write your answers on the lines. Use each term only once.

resources	renewable resources	reusable resources
nonrenewable resources		recycled

Dear Marsha,

Did you know that living things use materials called _____? Some of them will never be used up. We call them _____. Air, water, and the sun are good examples of these. There are also _____. These resources can be replaced. Replanting trees replaces cut trees. Some resources, like oil, coal, and metals, are _____. They cannot be replaced. We need to conserve these so we can use them longer. Some of these resources can be _____, or used again to make new products. Aluminum cans can be melted down and made into new cans.

Your friend,

Lisa

Harcourt

Name _____

Date _____

Write an Essay About Resources

Informative Writing—Compare and Contrast

Write a three-paragraph essay that compares and contrasts the three kinds of resources. For each paragraph's topic, answer these questions:

• How are these resources alike?
• How do they differ from one another?

Use the organizer below to help you plan your writing.

Paragraph Topics	Renewable Resources	Reusable Resources	Nonrenewable Resources
Paragraph 1: What are examples of each kind of resource?			
	How are these resources alike? How do they differ?		
Paragraph 2: How do people use these resources?			
	How are these uses alike? How do they differ?		
Paragraph 3: Are these resources endangered? If so, how?			
	How are these resources alike? How do they differ?		

Harcourt

Use with pages C110–C111.

Name _____ Date _____

The Water Cycle

LESSON 2
THE WATER CYCLE
How Water Changes and Moves

1. _____
Water changes
from a _____
to a _____ .

2. _____
Water changes
from a _____
to a _____ .

3. _____
Liquid water
falls to the
ground as _____ .

The Water Cycle
is the movement of water
_____
_____
_____

LESSON 1
WATER ON EARTH
Types of Water

8. _____
Where found
9. _____
10. _____
11. _____
Uses
12. _____
13. _____
14. _____

1. _____
Where found
2. _____
3. _____
4. _____
Uses
5. _____
6. _____
7. _____

15. Where salt and fresh water meet is called an
_____ .

Harcourt

Name _____

Date _____

Investigate Log

Land or Water

Materials

plastic inflatable globe

Activity Procedure

1 Work in groups of five. Choose one person to be the recorder. The other four people will toss the ball.

2 Have the four ball tossers stand in a circle. The recorder hands the ball to the first person, who gently tosses the ball to another person in the circle.

3 The catcher should catch the ball with open hands. Check to see if the tip of the catcher's right index finger is on land or water. The recorder should **record** this data.

4 Continue tossing and recording until the ball has been tossed 20 times.

5 Repeat Steps 3 and 4 two more times.

Harcourt

Investigate Log

Draw Conclusions

1. Total your counts. How many times did the catcher's right index finger touch water? Touch land? _____

_____

2. Where did the catcher's fingers land more often? Why do you think so?

_____

_____

3. **Scientists at Work** Scientists **use numbers** to **collect data**. Using your data, estimate how much of Earth's surface is covered by water.

_____

_____

Investigate Further You did this investigation 3 times. The more data you collect, the better your data becomes. How would doing the investigation 10 times change your data? Try it to find out.

_____

_____

Name _____

Date _____

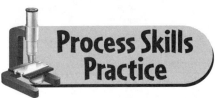

Collect Data and Use Numbers

When you collect data, you make observations and record them.
Using numbers helps you answer questions.

Think About Collecting Data and Using Numbers

You write to your cousin who lives in another state and tell her what a rainy
year it's been. She writes back and asks what you mean by "a rainy year." You
realize you need to collect data by finding out some rainfall measurements.
You look up the rainfall numbers for one month in the summer and one
month in the winter for this year and last year.

Rainfall in Summer and Winter	
August, this year	Week 1: 5 cm; Week 2: 7 cm; Week 3: 4 cm; Week 4: 2 cm
August, last year	Week 1: 3 cm; Week 2: 5 cm; Week 3: 2 cm; Week 4: 1 cm
February, this year	Week 1: 0 cm; Week 2: 2 cm; Week 3: 1 cm; Week 4: 3 cm
February, last year	Week 1: 0 cm; Week 2: 1 cm; Week 3: 0 cm; Week 4: 2 cm

1. How does collecting data by using numbers help you answer your

cousin's question? _____

_____

2. Why is it a good idea to collect rainfall totals for two months, instead

of just one? _____

3. Total the rainfall counts. How much rain fell in August of each year? How
much rain fell in February of each year? What is the total amount of rain
for each year? Was this year really rainy compared to last year?

_____

August, this year: _____   February, this year: _____   Total: _____

August, last year: _____   February, last year: _____   Total: _____

Summarize and Paraphrase a Selection

Read the selection about the Ogallala aquifer. Then fill in the chart with the main idea and supporting details in your own words.

The Ogallala Aquifer

An aquifer is a large area of groundwater. An aquifer has enough water to supply many wells. The Ogallala aquifer lies beneath part of northwestern Texas and a small part of eastern New Mexico. For over 100 years, the Ogallala has provided water to cities, towns, ranches, and farms. The Ogallala supplies 170,000 wells. Every year, more and more water is taken from the Ogallala. Currently, about 6 billion cubic meters of water is used a year. Unfortunately, nature cannot replace all of the water that is used. Water experts are encouraging people to conserve water. They hope this will help the aquifer last for many more years.

Main Idea	Supporting Details

Harcourt

Name _____

Date _____

Where Is Water Found on Earth?

Lesson Concept

More than two-thirds of Earth's surface is covered with water.
Most water on Earth is found in the oceans.

Vocabulary

groundwater (D8)   **estuary** (D12)

As you read the summary, fill in the blank with one of the vocabulary terms from above.

Without water there could be no life on Earth. Plants, animals, and people need water to live. Water is important to Earth's environment. Water helps cause winds and storms, and it changes the shape of Earth's surface. Only a small amount of Earth's water is fresh water. The rest is salt water found in the oceans. Water that is under Earth's surface is called

_____. There are places called _____ where fresh water and salt water meet.

Answer each question with one or more complete sentences.

1. What are some ways you could conserve, or save, water each day?

_____

_____

_____

2. Describe how groundwater gets under Earth's surface.

_____

_____

Name _____

Date _____

Investigate Log

Evaporation

Materials

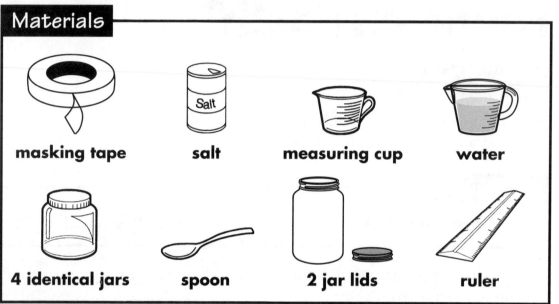

masking tape   salt   measuring cup   water

4 identical jars   spoon   2 jar lids   ruler

Activity Procedure

1 Put a strip of masking tape down the side of each jar.

2 Using the measuring cup, pour $\frac{1}{2}$ cup water into each jar. Stir a spoonful of salt into 2 of the jars. Mark these jars with an *S*. Mark the other 2 jars with an *F*.

3 Make a mark on the tape on each jar to show how high the water is. Then put the lids on one *S* jar and one *F* jar.

4 **Predict** from which jar the water will evaporate first. **Record** your prediction.

5 Place the jars in a sunny place.

6 **Observe** the jars every day for a week. Each day, mark how high the water in each jar is.

Harcourt

Name _____

Investigate Log

Draw Conclusions

1. Did all the water evaporate from any of the jars? If so, which one?

_____

2. Compare your prediction with your results. How did you make your

prediction? Was your prediction correct? _____

_____

_____

3. Scientists at Work To find the answers to some questions, scientists test
things that will change. These things are called *variables.* Then they add
something to the experiment that they know won't change. This is called
a *control.* What were the controls in this investigation?

_____

_____

Investigate Further Infer what would happen if you repeated the activity
but used different amounts of salt. How would the results change? Try the
activity to see if your inference was correct. Don't forget to use controls.

_____

Harcourt

Name _____

Date _____

Control Variables

Controlling variables is a way to make sure that experiments are fair tests. But before you can control variables, you have to know what the variables in your experiment are.

Think About Controlling Variables

Jessie wanted to do another investigation of water evaporation. She thought about the variables in her experiment. She came up with the following list.

Variable 1. the size of the water sample

Variable 2. the kind of water used

Variable 3. the shape of the container

Variable 4. the amount of time each sample was on the windowsill

Jessie wanted to control all but one variable, the shape of the container. She put one cup of water into a tall, thin drinking glass. Then she poured one cup of water into a cereal bowl. The water for both containers came from the same water bottle. Jessie placed the glass and the bowl on a sunny windowsill. She recorded her observations. Jessie noticed the water in the bowl evaporated more quickly than the water in the glass.

1. Why do you think the water evaporated more quickly from the bowl?

_____

_____

2. What would have happened if Jessie had controlled all but Variable 1?

_____

3. What would have happened if Jessie had controlled all but Variable 2?

_____

_____

Harcourt

Use with page D15.

Use Context to Determine/Confirm Word Meaning

How Water Changes

Look at the sentences below. Circle word clues or phrases that help define the underlined term. Write what you think the term means based on the clues. Then use the glossary in your science book or a dictionary to look up each term to check your answers.

1. The form that water takes depends on the amount of heat, or <u>thermal energy</u>, in it.

   _____

   _____

2. Water is in the air around you in the form of a gas you can't see called <u>water vapor</u>.

   _____

   _____

3. Heat must be added to a liquid to make it <u>evaporate</u>. Evaporation changes liquid water into water vapor.

   _____

   _____

4. During <u>condensation</u>, taking heat away from a gas, or cooling it, changes the gas into liquid.

   _____

   _____

Harcourt

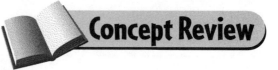

What Is the Water Cycle?

Lesson Concept

The water cycle is the movement of water from Earth's surface into the air and back to the surface again.

Vocabulary

evaporation (D17)   **condensation** (D17)

precipitation (D18)   **water cycle** (D18)

Underline the best answer.

1. The form water takes depends upon the amount of ____ in it.

A condensation **B** water vapor   **C** thermal energy   **D** gas

2. You pour a glass of soft drink and put some ice cubes in it. You leave the glass outside in the sun. The sun changes the ice into ____.

A liquid water   **B** condensation **C** water vapor   **D** evaporation

3. Earth uses the same water over and over again. The water you use today is ____ years old.

A 5,000   **B** 500   **C** 10,000   **D** billions of

Fill in the answers.

4. What three forms can water take? _____

_____

5. _____ is the changing of a liquid into gas.

6. _____ is the changing of a gas into a liquid.

7. _____ is water that falls to Earth as rain, snow, sleet, or hail.

8. _____ is the movement of water into the air and back again.

Harcourt

Name _____

Date _____

Recognize Vocabulary

In the space provided, write the letter of the term in Column B that best fits the definition in Column A. Use each term only once.

Column A

_____ **1.** Rain that soaks into soil and rocks

_____ **2.** Where fresh water mixes with salt water

_____ **3.** Changing of a liquid to a gas

_____ **4.** Water that falls from the sky to Earth

_____ **5.** Changing of a gas to a liquid

_____ **6.** Movement of water from Earth's surface into air and back to Earth's surface again

Column B

A evaporation

B condensation

C precipitation

D water cycle

E estuary

F groundwater

Choose two of the vocabulary words from Column B. Then, using your own words, write a sentence that uses each word correctly.

_____

_____

_____

_____

_____

_____

Harcourt

Tell a Story from the Water Cycle

Narrative Writing—First-person Story

Imagine that you are a raindrop or a snowflake. Tell the story of your life. Use what you know about the water cycle to make your story accurate and interesting. The story map below will help you plan your narrative.

Character (raindrop or snowflake):	Setting (climate region):
Where does your story begin?	
What happens to make you a raindrop or a snowflake?	
What do you see on your journey?	
Where does your story end?	

Harcourt

Chapter 2 • Graphic Organizer for Chapter Concepts

Observing Weather

LESSON 1
WEATHER

Properties of Air

1. _____

2. _____

3. _____

LESSON 2
MEASURING WEATHER

What Is Measured and
How It Is Measured

1. _____ is measured with a _____

2. _____ is measured with a rain gauge or snow board.

3. _____ is measured with a _____ and an _____

LESSON 3
FORECASTING WEATHER

How Data Is Gathered

1. _____

2. _____

3. _____

4. _____

Things Shown on a Weather Map

1. _____

2. _____

3. _____

4. _____

Properties of Air

Materials

plastic container   water   paper towel

plastic cup   index card

Activity Procedure

Part A

1 Half-fill the plastic container with water.

2 Crumple the paper towel. Push it to the bottom of the plastic cup.

3 Turn the cup upside down. Push the cup to the bottom of the plastic container. Do not tilt the cup as you are pushing it downward. Then pull the cup straight up and out of the water. **Observe** the paper towel. **Record** your observations.

Part B

4 Remove the paper towel from the cup. Half-fill the cup with water. Put the index card over the cup opening.

5 Hold the cup over the plastic container. Use your right hand to hold the cup and your left hand to hold the index card in place. Quickly turn the cup over. Take your left hand off the index card. **Record** your observations.

Harcourt

Name _____

Draw Conclusions

1. What did you **observe** in Part A? _____

_____

2. What did you **observe** in Part B? _____

_____

3. **Scientists at Work** Scientists **observe** things that happen all around them. They use their observations to **infer** why those things happen. Use your observations to infer one property of air for each part of this investigation. _____

_____

_____

_____

Investigate Further Suppose you repeat Part B with a cup that is almost filled with water. **Predict** what will happen. Then try it. _____

_____

Harcourt

Name _____

Date _____

Observe and Infer

When you observe, you use your senses to examine things. Then you can record what you observe.

Think About Observing and Inferring

Suppose you do the following investigation. You put a funnel in the neck of a glass bottle. You fill the space around the funnel with modeling clay, making sure the clay is packed tightly. You pour water slowly into the funnel. You observe that no water goes into the bottle. Then you repeat the experiment. This time you pour water into the funnel, almost to the top. Then you carefully use a nail to poke a hole through the clay to the inside of the bottle. Now water flows through the funnel into the bottle.

1. In the first experiment, you observed that no water flowed through the funnel. Why do you think this is so? _____

   _____

2. What do you think this shows about air? _____

   _____

3. In the second experiment, you observed that no water flowed into the bottle until you poked a hole in the clay. Why do you think the water could flow into the bottle? _____

   _____

   _____

   _____

4. What inference could you make about the purpose of the clay?

   _____

   _____

   _____

   _____

Harcourt

Use with page D29.

Name _____

Date _____

Use Context to Determine/Confirm Word Meaning

Kinds of Storms

Weather changes all the time. Weather is what is happening in the atmosphere at a certain place. Many kinds of storms happen in different weather systems. Blizzards are large snowstorms. They have low temperatures and strong winds. Often there is so much snow blowing that it is hard to see. Hurricanes also have strong winds. But hurricanes form over warm ocean waters and usually travel over open ocean or along coastlines. A tornado is a violent windstorm with winds so strong that they can destroy buildings and lift cars right off the ground! Ice storms are very dangerous. During an ice storm, freezing rain falls to Earth and freezes immediately. When the ice builds up, it can make road surfaces slick and travel dangerous.

1. What are some word clues that help you know what a blizzard is?

_____

2. What are some word clues that help you know what a hurricane is?

_____

3. What are some word clues that help you know what a tornado is?

_____

4. What are some word clues that help you know what an ice storm is?

_____

Harcourt

What Is Weather?

Lesson Concept

Weather is what is happening in the atmosphere at a certain place.

Vocabulary

atmosphere (D30)   **weather** (D32)

Write your answers to the questions.

1. What are the three properties of air? _____

_____

2. What do meteorologists do? _____

_____

_____

3. How does the atmosphere help Earth? _____

_____

_____

Underline the best answer.

4. What absorbs harmful rays from the sun?
   A atmosphere   **B** troposphere   **C** ozone   **D** air particles

5. Weather takes place in ____.
   A the air layer farthest away from Earth
   B the air layer closest to Earth

Harcourt

Measuring Temperature

Materials

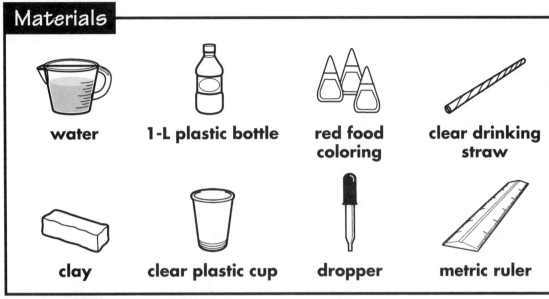

water **1-L plastic bottle** **red food coloring** **clear drinking straw**

clay **clear plastic cup** **dropper** **metric ruler**

Activity Procedure

1 Put water in the bottle until it is almost full. Add 10 drops of food coloring.

2 Put the straw in the bottle. Three-fourths of the straw should stick out of the bottle. Seal the opening around the straw with clay.

3 Half-fill the cup with water. Add three drops of food coloring.

4 Use the dropper to put water from the cup into the straw. Add water until you can see the water in the straw above the clay stopper.

5 Make a mark at the water level in the straw. You have made a thermometer. The higher the level of liquid in the straw, the higher the temperature.

6 Take the thermometer to five different places at school. Leave it at each place for 15 minutes. Use a ruler to **measure** the water level in the straw from the mark to the top of the water level. Do not squeeze the bottle while you measure. **Record** the measurement and the location.

Harcourt

Draw Conclusions

1. What happened to the water levels in the straw in the different locations?

   _____

   _____

   _____

   _____

2. What information could you learn by using your thermometer?

   _____

   _____

   _____

   What information is impossible to learn by using your thermometer?

   _____

   _____

   _____

3. **Scientists at Work** Scientists sometimes **use numbers** to put things in order. Look at the numbers you recorded. Use the numbers to order the

   locations from warmest to coolest. _____

   _____

   _____

   _____

Harcourt

Name _____

Date _____

Use Numbers and Compare

You can use numbers to put things in order and to compare one set of things to another.

Think About Using Numbers and Comparing

At science camp in August, Jane and two other campers made thermometers like the one you made in the investigation. On a hot day, they took their thermometers to three different places outside. After fifteen minutes, they checked their thermometers. They had a surprise! The water had risen to the same level on each thermometer. All the temperatures were the same. Then they took their thermometers to three different places inside the dining hall. This time the water was at a different level on each thermometer.

1. How did the campers know the temperatures were the same in the first

three locations? _____

_____

2. Why do you think the water level was the same on each thermometer at

the first location? _____

_____

3. What did the water levels tell them at the second location, inside the

dining hall? _____

_____

4. Imagine that you were at science camp. Where would you choose to leave

your thermometer? _____

_____

5. Predict the temperature at the location you chose. Will it be warm or

cool? Explain. _____

_____

Harcourt

Use with page D35.

Summarize and Paraphrase a Selection

Read the selection below. Write the main idea of the paragraph on the lines below. Then use your own words to write captions for each picture to help summarize the selection.

Wind

Wind is the movement of air. Wind can be helpful. It can cool you on a hot day, or it can help you fly a kite. Wind can blow away pollution from the air. Some days it may feel as if there is no wind! Sometimes having not enough wind can be frustrating. A sailboat doesn't get very far when there isn't much wind. It may make things difficult when winds are strong, but people still manage. Often, just walking on a windy day can be difficult. It may be hard to keep your hat and coat on! A strong wind in a rainstorm can turn an umbrella inside out. Unfortunately, winds also can be very damaging. During strong storms such as tornadoes, wind can knock trees over and even destroy buildings.

Main Idea: _____

_____

_____

_____

_____

_____

Harcourt

How Are Weather Conditions Measured?

Weather conditions are measured with tools such as thermometers, rain gauges, and anemometers.

Vocabulary

temperature (D36)	**front** (D37)
anemometer (D40)	**wind** (D40)

Read the summary. Then answer the questions that follow.

Temperature is a measure of how warm or cold something is. Air temperature is always changing. A large body of air with the same temperature and moisture is called an air mass. Precipitation is any kind of water that falls from the sky. Meteorologists use rain gauges and snow boards to measure precipitation. Wind is the movement of air. A tool called an anemometer is used to measure wind speed.

Underline the best answer.

1. Thermometers can be used to measure ____.

   A temperature   **B** rainfall   **C** air pressure   **D** wind speed

2. A large body of air with the same temperature and moisture is called ____.

   A a front   **B** a cloud   **C** air pressure   **D** an air mass

3. An anemometer measures ____.

   A air pressure **B** precipitation **C** wind speed   **D** flood possibilities

4. Rain gauges and snow boards are used to measure ____.

   A air pressure **B** precipitation **C** moisture   **D** rainfall

Reading Weather Maps

Materials

weather map

Activity Procedure

1 Study the weather map and the key to the symbols that it uses.

2 Use the map to answer the questions.

Harcourt

Name _____

Draw Conclusions

1. Where is there a thunderstorm? _____

2. Find the cold front. What can you tell about the weather along the

cold front? _____

_____

_____

3. Scientists at Work Scientists **interpret data** on weather maps to learn
about the weather in different places. Interpret data on this map to

describe the weather in Minneapolis, Minnesota. _____

_____

_____

_____

Investigate Further The weather in the United States generally moves from
west to east. Imagine that you are in New York City. Use the data on the map
to **predict** what your weather may be like about one week from now.

_____

_____

_____

_____

_____

Harcourt

Name _____

Date _____

Interpret Data

Data is information given to you or information that you gather during activities. When you interpret data, you decide what it means.

Think About Interpreting Data

The table that follows shows a daily weather report for five days. Interpret the data, and answer the questions that follow.

Daily Weather Report			
Day	**Temperature**	**Precipitation**	**Precipitation Symbol**
Monday	29°C (84° F)	Rain	
Tuesday	26°C (79° F)	Rain	
Wednesday	24°C (75° F)	Sunny	
Thursday	26°C (79° F)	Fog	
Friday	29°C (84° F)	Thunderstorm	

1. What was the coolest day? _____

2. On which days did it rain? _____

3. Compare the weather on Monday and on Wednesday. Which day would have been better for outdoor exercise? Explain your answer.

_____

_____

4. Which day would have been the worst day to be outside? Explain.

_____

5. Use the symbols you learned in the investigation to fill in the last column of the table.

Harcourt

Name _____

Date _____

Use Graphic Sources for Information

Use the information from the map to answer the questions below.

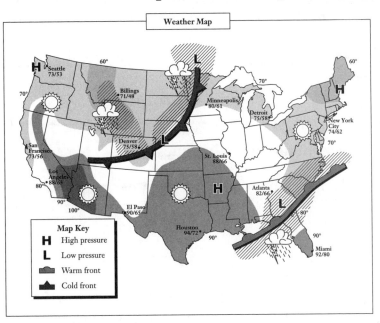

1. How high might the temperature reach in San Francisco?

_____

2. What kind of pressure system is in Seattle?

_____

3. Name two things that describe the weather south of Atlanta.

_____

4. What is the expected low temperature in Minneapolis?

_____

5. What city had a cold front and low-pressure system pass through it?

_____

6. Which city is showing the highest temperature?

_____

Harcourt

Name _____

Date _____

What Is a Weather Map?

Lesson Concept

There are a number of ways to gather weather data. A weather map uses symbols to show weather conditions over large areas.

Vocabulary

weather map (D46)

Write your answers to the following questions.

1. List four kinds of weather data that a weather map shows.

_____

_____

_____

2. List four ways that information about weather is gathered.

_____

_____

Underline the best answer.

3. Weather balloons gather data on temperature, precipitation, and ____.

   A clouds and storms   **C** wind

   B ocean temperatures   **D** storms

4. Weather data collected by the National Weather Service goes into computers that organize the information into ____.

   A maps   **C** rain chances

   B cloud readings   **D** storm warnings

Harcourt

Use with page D47.

Name _____

Date _____

Recognize Vocabulary

Read each sentence. Find the missing term in the box below.
Write the correct term on the line.

weather map	anemometer	wind	temperature
precipitation	atmosphere	front	weather

1. A map that shows weather data for a large area is called a

   _____.

2. The air that surrounds Earth is the _____.

3. An _____ is a tool that measures wind speed.

4. An occurrence that happens in the atmosphere at a certain place is called

   _____.

5. Any kind of water that falls to Earth is _____.

6. _____ is a measure of how warm or cold
   something is.

7. The movement of air is _____.

8. A place where two air masses of different temperatures meet is a

   _____.

Harcourt

Name _____

Date _____

Explain a Thunderstorm

Informative Writing—Explanation

Imagine that you are helping out at a summer camp for younger children. The children may be frightened by thunderstorms. Write a short speech that you could give to younger children, explaining how a thunderstorm happens. Use colorful words to catch the children's imagination. Complete the outline below to help you plan your speech.

Step 1: What happens when a cold front hits warm air?

Step 2: What makes a thunderhead form?

Step 3: What happens when air moves rapidly up and down?

Step 4: Which comes first—thunder or lightning?

Step 5: What happens when the air cools?

Harcourt

Name _____ Date _____

Earth and Its Place in the Solar System

LESSON 1
WHAT IS THE SOLAR SYSTEM?

Inner Planets

1. _____
2. _____
3. _____
4. _____

Outer Planets

5. _____
6. _____
7. _____
8. _____
9. _____

Other Objects in the Solar System

10. _____
11. _____

LESSON 2
WHAT CAUSES EARTH'S SEASONS?

Movement of Earth in Space

1. _____
2. _____

Seasons

3. caused by Earth's _____ around the sun

Day and night

4. caused by Earth's _____ on its axis

LESSON 3
HOW DO THE MOON AND EARTH INTERACT?

Phases of the Moon

1. _____
2. _____
3. _____
4. _____

Eclipses

5. Lunar eclipses are caused by _____ casting a shadow on the _____

6. Solar eclipses are caused by the _____ casting a shadow on _____

Name _____

Date _____

The Planets

Materials

pencil

planet picture cards (optional)

paper

Planet Data			
Planet	**Distance from Sun (in millions of kilometers)**	**Distance Across (in kilometers)**	**Length of Year (y = Earth year) (d = Earth day)**
Earth	150	12,750	365 d
Jupiter	778	143,000	12 y
Mars	228	6,800	2 y
Mercury	58	4,900	88 d
Neptune	4,505	49,000	165 y
Pluto	5,890	2,300	248 y
Saturn	1,427	120,000	29 y
Uranus	2,869	51,000	84 y
Venus	108	12,000	225 d

Activity Procedure

1 Record your answers in the Ordering Planet Data Chart on the next page.

2 **Use numbers** from the data table to find each planet's distance from the sun. **Record** in your chart the names of the planets, beginning with the one closest to the sun.

3 **Use numbers** from the data table to find the distance across each planet. The planet with the shortest distance across is the smallest planet. Use numbers to **order** the planets by size. **Record** the names of the planets in order, beginning with the smallest planet.

Harcourt

Name _____

Ordering Planet Data		
Closest to the Sun to Farthest from the Sun	**Smallest to Largest**	**Shortest Year to Longest Year**

Draw Conclusions

1. Which planet is closest to the sun? Farthest away? _____

_____

2. Which is the largest planet? The smallest? _____

3. **Scientists at Work** Scientists sometimes **use numbers** to put things in **order**. Scientists have studied the same data you used in this

investigation. _____

_____

_____

Investigate Further Plan and conduct an experiment that **makes a model** to show one set of your planet data. You may wish to use the planet picture cards in your model.

Harcourt

Name _____

Date _____

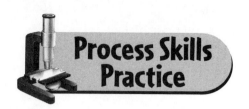

Use Numbers

You can use numbers to order things and put them into groups.

Think About Using Numbers

Suppose you want to group the planets in a number of different ways. Look at the table that follows.

Planet	Distance Across (in kilometers)
Earth	12,750
Jupiter	143,000
Mars	6,800
Mercury	4,900
Neptune	49,000
Pluto	2,300
Saturn	120,000
Uranus	51,000
Venus	12,000

1. Study the distance across each planet. Group the four largest planets together. _____

_____

2. Now study the distances across again, and group the five smallest planets together. _____

_____

Harcourt

Use with page D57.

Name _____

Date _____

Use Prefixes and Suffixes to Determine Word Meaning

Read the sentences below. Then determine which word in each sentence contains a prefix or a suffix. Write the word, the root word, and a definition below the sentence.

1. Jupiter is the largest planet in our solar system.

Word: _____

Root word: _____

Definition of word: _____

2. Mercury is the hottest planet in our solar system.

Word: _____

Root word: _____

Definition of word: _____

3. Mars is colder than Earth.

Word: _____

Root word: _____

Definition of word: _____

Harcourt

Concept Review

What Is the Solar System?

Lesson Concept

The solar system has nine planets that orbit the sun. Earth is one of those planets. Asteroids and comets are also parts of the solar system.

Vocabulary

solar system (D58)	**orbit** (D58)	**planet** (D58)
asteroid (D64)	**comet** (D64)	

As you read the summary, fill in the blanks with vocabulary terms.

An _____ is the path an object takes as it moves

around another object in space. A _____ is a large body
of rock or gas that orbits the sun. There are nine planets in the

_____. Earth is one of those planets. The sun is the
center of the solar system. It is a star made of hot, glowing gases. The

sun is closer to Earth than other stars are. _____

and _____ are also parts of the solar system.

Follow the directions for each question.

1. List three ways that Earth is different from the other inner planets.

_____

_____

2. List three ways the outer planets are alike. _____

_____

_____

_____

_____

Harcourt

Name _____

Date _____

How Sunlight Strikes Earth

Materials

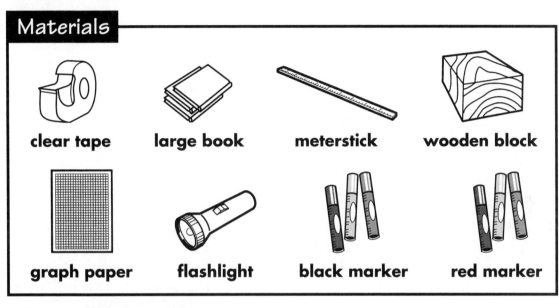

clear tape	**large book**	**meterstick**	**wooden block**
graph paper	**flashlight**	**black marker**	**red marker**

Activity Procedure

1 Tape the graph paper to the book.

2 Hold the flashlight about 50 cm above the book. Shine the light straight down. The beam will make a circle on the paper. If the circle is bigger than the paper, bring the light closer.

3 Have a partner use the black marker to draw around the light beam on the paper.

4 **Observe** the brightness of the light on the squares. **Record** your observations.

5 Keep the flashlight in the same position. Have a partner put the block under one end of the book and use the red marker to draw around the light on the paper.

6 **Observe** the brightness on the squares again. **Record** your observations.

Name _____

Draw Conclusions

1. How many squares are inside the black line? How many squares are inside the red line? _____

_____

_____

_____

_____

2. Inside which line was the light brighter? _____

_____

_____

3. **Scientists at Work** Scientists **compare** things to find out how they are the same and how they are different. Compare the results of Steps 3 and 5 of the investigation. Do straight light rays or tilted light rays give stronger light? Suppose the paper is Earth's surface. The light is the sun.

Which area would have warmer weather? Explain. _____

_____

_____

_____

Investigate Further Form a hypothesis about what will happen if the book is tilted even more. **Plan and conduct an experiment** to test your

hypothesis. _____

_____

_____

Harcourt

Name _____

Date _____

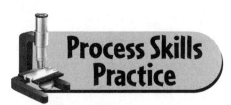

Compare

When you compare, you observe the properties of two or more things to see how they are alike and how they are different.

Think About Comparing

In September, Jean hung a picture of her favorite gymnast on the wall of her room. She hung it in a spot where the sun would shine on it at 3:00 P.M. each day, just when she sat down to do her homework. One day Jean noticed that the sun wasn't shining on her picture anymore. It was shining on her wall next to the picture. Jean thought this was interesting. She taped a circle of paper on the wall where the sun shone. She put the date and time on the paper. The next week, the sun was shining lower on the wall. She taped another circle of paper where the sun shone. Once a week she saw the sunny spot was lower on the wall and taped a circle of paper where the sun shone. She put the time and date on each circle of paper. By January 1, Jean had 16 circles of paper taped to her wall.

1. What did Jean observe about the sunny spot? _____

_____

2. What two things could Jean compare? _____

_____

_____

3. How else could Jean record her observations and comparisons?

_____

_____

_____

4. What could Jean infer from her observations? _____

_____

_____

Harcourt

Name _____

Date _____

Use Graphic Sources for Information

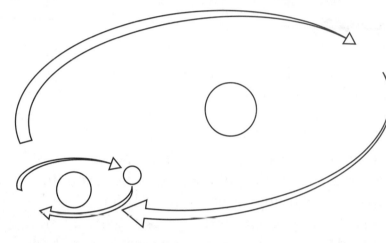

Both Earth and the moon rotate. Earth rotates once a day. The moon rotates about once a month.

Write *True* or *False* next to each statement. If the statement is false, rewrite it to make it true.

1. Earth revolves around the sun.

_____

_____

2. The sun revolves around the moon.

_____

_____

3. Earth and the moon both revolve around the sun.

_____

_____

4. The moon remains still as it revolves around the Earth.

_____

_____

Harcourt

Name _____

Date _____

Concept Review

What Causes Earth's Seasons?

Lesson Concept

Earth has seasons because its axis is tilted. This means the sun heats Earth's surface differently at different times of the year.

Vocabulary

rotation (D68)   **axis** (D68)   **revolution** (D68)

Underline the correct answer.

1. Earth rotates. Rotation is ____.

   A a revolution   **B** the spinning of an   **C** a season
                              object on its axis

2. Earth makes revolutions around the sun. Earth's revolution takes ____.

   A one year   **B** a lunar year   **C** three months in
                                                   summer

3. Earth's axis is tilted. If Earth's axis were not tilted there would be ____.

   A only three   **B** seasons every   **C** no seasons
       seasons   other year

4. Seasons in the northern and southern halves of Earth are ____.

   A reversed   **B** the same   **C** moving

5. For part of the year, the North Pole points in the direction of the sun. This occurs during ____ in the Northern Hemisphere.

   A winter   **B** winter and   **C** summer
                        summer

Harcourt

Use with page D73.

The Moon's Phases

Materials

lamp with no shade

softball

Activity Procedure

1 Work with a partner. Turn on the lamp. Your teacher will darken the room.

2 Have person 1 hold the ball and stand with his or her back to the lighted bulb. Hold the ball as shown on page D75. Continue holding the ball this way until the end of the procedure.

3 Have person 2 stand in position 1. **Observe** the ball. Make a drawing of the ball's lighted side.

4 Person 2 now moves to position 2. Turn toward the ball. Make a drawing of the lighted part of the ball.

5 Have person 2 move to position 3. Make a drawing of the lighted part of the ball.

6 Person 2 again moves, this time to position 4. Turn toward the ball. Make a drawing of the lighted part of the ball.

7 Switch roles and repeat the procedure so person 1 can observe the patterns of light on the ball.

Harcourt

Name _____

Draw Conclusions

1. What part of the ball was lighted at each position? _____

_____

_____

_____

2. The ball represents the moon. What does the light bulb represent? What

represents a person viewing the moon from Earth? _____

_____

_____

3. Scientists at Work Scientists **use models** to make **inferences** to explain
how things work. If the ball represents the moon, what can you infer that

the different parts of the lighted ball represent? _____

_____

Harcourt

Name _____

Date _____

Observe and Infer

When you observe, you use your senses to gather information.

Think About Observing and Inferring

One night Isaac looked out his window and saw a big moon in the sky. He wanted to get some information about the moon by observing it. He went out every night to see how the moon had changed. He drew a picture each night for four weeks. Every night he saw a small change in how the moon looked. He made notes about what he observed. Here are some of the notes Isaac made.

OCT. 5
BIG, BIG MOON

OCT. 12
MOON LOOKS
HALF GONE

OCT. 15
NOW ITS EVEN
SMALLER, LESS
THAN HALF

OCT. 18 A LITTLE,
TINY, SLIVER

1. What observations did he make of the moon? _____

_____

_____

2. How could Isaac learn more about the moon through observations?

_____

_____

_____

_____

3. What inference could you make about why the moon looked different

over the time period of Isaac's observations? _____

_____

Harcourt

Name _____

Date _____

Identify Cause and Effect

Earth, Moon, and Sun

Underline the causes and circle the effects in the following sentences.

1. When the sun shines on an object, the object casts a shadow.

2. When Earth's shadow falls on the moon, a lunar eclipse happens.

3. A total lunar eclipse makes all of the moon's face look dark red.

4. A solar eclipse happens when the moon's shadow falls on Earth.

5. When a total eclipse occurs, the whole sky turns dark in the middle of

the day.

Identify the cause and effect shown in the picture.

Cause: _____

Effect: _____

Harcourt

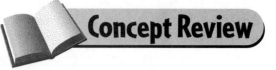

How Do the Moon and Earth Interact?

Lesson Concept

Phases are the different shapes the moon seems to have in the sky. The moon goes through its phases every $29\frac{1}{2}$ days.

Vocabulary

phase (D76)   **lunar eclipse** (D78)   **solar eclipse** (D80)

As you read the summary, fill in each blank with a vocabulary term.

The half of the moon that faces the sun is always lighted. As the moon moves around Earth, different parts of its lighted and dark sides face Earth. The moon's phase depends on the part of the lighted half that can be seen. The different shapes the moon seems to have in the sky are called

_____. There are solar and lunar eclipses. A _____.

happens when the moon's shadow falls on Earth. A _____ happens when Earth's shadow falls on the moon.

Circle the term that best completes the sentence.

1. The half of the moon that faces the sun is always _____.

   A dark   **B** lighted

2. _____ are the different shapes the moon seems to have.

   A Phases   **B** Rotations

3. A lunar eclipse happens when Earth's _____ falls on the moon.

   A shadow   **B** atmosphere

4. The moon's shadow falling on Earth is the cause of a _____ eclipse.

   A solar   **B** lunar

Harcourt

Recognize Vocabulary

**The vocabulary terms that follow are not correctly defined.
Write the correct meaning for each term.**

1. solar system—the moon and objects that revolve around it

_____

_____

2. orbit—the path of the sun _____

_____

_____

3. planet—a large body of fire that orbits the sun _____

_____

_____

4. asteroid—a shooting star _____

_____

_____

5. comet—a large ball of dust and ice that orbits the moon

_____

_____

6. rotation—the spinning of an object in space _____

_____

_____

7. Earth's axis—an actual line that goes through the North and South Poles

_____

_____

Harcourt

Name _____

Date _____

Explain a Solar Eclipse

Informative Writing–Explanation

Imagine that you are able to communicate with people living thousands of
years ago. They ask you to explain what really happens during a solar
eclipse. Write a simple explanation, and illustrate it with drawings. Use the
outline below to help you plan your writing.

Words	Pictures
What causes a solar eclipse?	
What happens on Earth during a solar eclipse?	
In the beginning:	
At the peak of the eclipse:	
After the eclipse peaks:	
How can you stay safe during a solar eclipse?	

Use with pages D86–D87.

Chapter 1 • Graphic Organizer for Chapter Concepts

Properties of Matter

LESSON 1
PHYSICAL PROPERTIES

Three Physical Properties of Matter:

1. _____

2. _____

3. _____

Three States of Matter:

4. _____

5. _____

6. _____

LESSON 2
SOLIDS, LIQUIDS, AND GASES

1. Matter is made of _____.

Changing States of Matter

2. Adding heat changes a solid to a _____.

3. Adding heat changes a liquid to a _____.

4. Taking away heat from a gas changes it to a _____.

5. Taking away heat from a liquid changes it to a _____.

LESSON 3
MEASURING MATTER

1. The amount of space that matter takes up is its _____.

2. The amount of matter in an object is its _____.

Physical Properties

Materials

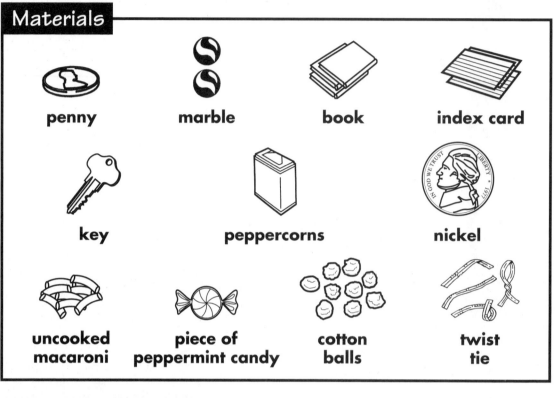

penny

marble

book

index card

key

peppercorns

nickel

uncooked macaroni

piece of peppermint candy

cotton balls

twist tie

Activity Procedure

1 Make charts like those on the next page.

2 Look at the objects you have been given. Notice whether they look shiny or dull. Notice how many colors each one has. **Record** your **observations**.

3 Touch the objects. Feel whether the objects are hard or soft. Feel whether they are rough or smooth. **Record** your **observations**.

4 Next, tap each object lightly with your fingernail. What kind of sound does it make? **Record** your **observations**.

5 Smell each object. **Record** your **observations**.

Harcourt

Name _____   **Investigate Log**

Object	How It Looks			How It Feels			
	Shiny	Dull	Color	Hard	Soft	Rough	Smooth

Object	How It Smells			How It Sounds			
	Sweet	Sharp	No Smell	Loud	Soft	Makes a Ping	No Sound

Draw Conclusions

1. Which objects are hard and rough? _____

   Which objects are hard and smooth? _____

   Which objects are soft and rough? _____

   Which objects are soft and smooth? _____

2. **Compare** your chart with the chart of another group. Are any objects in

   different columns? Why? _____

   _____

   _____

3. **Scientists at Work** Scientists learn about the world by **observing** with
   their five senses. Which of the five senses did you not use in the

   investigation? _____

   Investigate Further form a hypothesis About how physical properties
   change with the size of the sample. **Plan and conduct an experiment** to test
   your hypothesis.

Harcourt

Name _____

Date _____

Observe and Record

You use your senses to observe the world around you. As you make observations, you can record your data by writing it down.

Think About Observing and Recording

Dmitri asked his friend Rosa, a chef, to give a talk at his kitchen supply store. Rosa spoke to Dmitri's customers about preparing a meal properly. Rosa told the customers that when she shops, she looks carefully at everything she buys to be sure it is fresh. She lightly squeezes a package of bread to be sure it is not hard and stale. Even while she is preparing the food, she continues to observe it. When she washes the lettuce for salad, she feels it to be sure it is crisp. After the food is cooked, Rosa tastes it to see if she needs to add salt. She also looks at the food on the plate to be sure it looks good.

1. What senses does Rosa use to observe the food? _____

_____

2. How do Rosa's observations help her prepare a meal?

_____

_____

3. Suppose you had these foods for lunch. For each food, circle the observation to record what you would expect.

Food	Observation	
Peanut Butter	bitter	salty
Bread	fresh	stale
Celery	soft	crunchy
Cookies	sour	sweet

Harcourt

Name _____

Date _____

Compare and Contrast

Read about different kinds of matter in the following sentences. Then tell what is being compared in each sentence, and tell whether the things are alike or different.

Matter

1. Both a horse and a dog are made of matter, but a horse is much larger than a dog.

   What is being compared? _____ and _____

   Are they alike or different? _____

2. The fur on a slipper feels soft, but the sole is hard and smooth.

   What is being compared? _____ and _____

   Are they alike or different? _____

3. Putty and clay are both things that can bend.

   What is being compared? _____ and _____

   Are they alike or different? _____

4. A skunk has an unpleasant odor, but a lilac usually has a nice scent.

   What is being compared? _____ and _____

   Are they alike or different? _____

Harcourt

Use with page E8.

What Are Physical Properties of Matter?

Lesson Concept

Matter has many physical properties that you can observe by using your five senses.

Vocabulary

matter (E6)	**physical property** (E6)	**solid** (E11)
gas (E12)	**liquid** (E12)	

Answer the following questions about matter.

1. John and Tony go to the circus. They see a lion, a giraffe, and an elephant.

John, Tony, and the animals are matter because they _____.

A take up space   **B** are breathing   **C** are at the circus

2. John and Tony observe a tall clown on stilts and a tiny clown riding a tricycle. One clown has pink hair. Another clown wears a very large fake nose. What physical properties do John and Tony observe with their

sense of sight? _____

A smell and color   **B** taste and feel   **C** size and color

3. Tony smells something good. It's popcorn! Tony and John get bags of salty, buttery popcorn and cups of sweet pink lemonade. Taste and smell are physical properties of matter. Which words describe these senses?

_____

A soft and fuzzy   **B** light and dark   **C** sweet and salty

4. John buys Tony helium balloons to take home from the circus. In which

state of matter is the helium inside the balloon? _____

A gas   **B** solid   **C** liquid

Harcourt

One Way Matter Can Change

Materials

clear plastic cup   2 ice cubes   paper towel   marker

Activity Procedure

1 Place the plastic cup on the paper towel. Put the ice cubes in the cup.

2 **Form a hypothesis** about what will happen to the ice cubes after 45 minutes.

_____

_____

3 **Observe** what's in the cup after 45 minutes. **Record** what you see.

_____

Was your hypothesis correct? _____

4 Mark the outside of the cup to show how high the water is. **Predict** what you will see inside the cup in the morning if you leave it out all night. Then leave the cup sitting out.

My prediction: _____

_____

5 **Observe** the cup the next morning. **Record** what you see.

_____

_____

Harcourt

Draw Conclusions

1. What do you think caused the ice to change? _____

_____

_____

2. What do you think happened to the water when you left it out all night?

_____

_____

_____

3. **Scientists at Work** Scientists form **hypotheses** based on things they have **observed** before. What had you observed before that helped you

make your predictions? _____

_____

_____

Investigate Further **Plan and conduct an experiment** to test this **hypothesis:** water freezes faster than orange juice. _____

_____

_____

Harcourt

Name _____

Date _____

Hypothesize

Read the paragraph below. Make a hypothesis about what might happen next.

Winter Pond

As winter comes and the temperature drops, the water in the pond changes from one state to another. When the temperature drops below 0°C (32° F), the water changes from liquid water to solid ice. It will stay ice until the temperature rises above 0°C.

What will happen to the water when spring comes? Write your hypothesis on the lines below.

_____

_____

_____

Harcourt

Use with page E15.

Name _____

Date _____

Use Prefixes and Suffixes to Determine Word Meaning

A prefix or a suffix can change the meaning of a word. For each root word below, add the suffixes from the list in each box. Write whether the new word is a noun or a verb. Then write a definition for each new word.

Suffixes

-ion the word becomes a noun
-ing the word becomes part of a verb

1. Root word: evaporate
new word: _____
noun or verb: _____
definition: _____

new word: _____
noun or verb: _____
definition: _____

2. Root word: connect
new word: _____
noun or verb: _____
definition: _____

new word: _____
noun or verb: _____
definition: _____

Harcourt

What Are Solids, Liquids, and Gases?

Lesson Concept

Atoms are small particles that make up matter. Whether matter is a solid, liquid, or gas depends on how tightly atoms fit together.

Vocabulary

atom (E16)   **evaporation** (E18)

Put a check mark in front of the statement in each pair that agrees with what you have learned.

_____ **1.** The atoms of solids do not move very much.

_____   The atoms of solids can slide past each other.

_____ **2.** Gas particles stick together tightly.

_____   Gas particles are not connected to each other and are not close to each other.

_____ **3.** Particles of liquid are more loosely attached than those in a solid. The particles can slide past each other.

_____   Particles of liquid are like those in a solid.

_____ **4.** The state of matter can be changed by adding or taking away heat.

_____   The state of matter can be changed by touching the particles.

_____ **5.** Gas particles are the basic building blocks of matter.

_____   Atoms are the basic building blocks of matter.

Harcourt

Measuring Mass and Volume

Materials

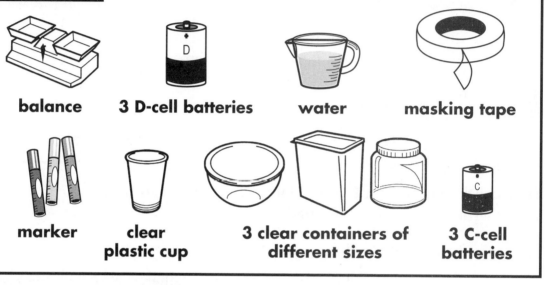

balance   3 D-cell batteries   water   masking tape

marker   clear plastic cup   3 clear containers of different sizes   3 C-cell batteries

Activity Procedure

Part A

1 Put a C-cell in the pan on the left side of the balance. Put a D-cell in the pan on the right side. **Record** which battery is heavier.

2 Add C-cells to the left side and D-cells to the right side until the pans are balanced. You may need to use some of the small masses from the balance to make the cells balance perfectly. **Record** the number of C-cells and D-cells you use.

Part B

3 Fill the cup half-full with water. Use a piece of tape to mark how high the water is in the cup. **Predict** how high the water will be in each container if you pour the water into it. Mark each prediction with a piece of tape. Write P (for prediction) on the tape.

4 Pour the water into the next container. Mark the height of the water with a piece of tape. Write *A* (for *Actual*) on the tape.

Harcourt

5 Repeat Step 4 for each of the other containers.

Draw Conclusions

1. **Compare** the numbers of C-cells and D-cells it took to balance the pans. **Draw a conclusion** from these numbers about the masses of the batteries.

_____

_____

_____

2. Describe the height of the water in each container. Why did the same amount of water look different in the different containers?

_____

_____

_____

_____

3. **Scientists at Work** Scientists **measure** matter by using tools that are marked with standard amounts. What was the standard amount you used

in this activity to measure the water? _____

_____

Measure

Measuring is a way to observe and compare things accurately. You can use an instrument like a ruler or a balance to measure the object.

Think About Measuring

Tina brought two boxes of cookies to class. One box was larger than the other. She invited three classmates to look at the boxes and predict which had more mass. Two classmates chose the larger box. She put the two boxes on the balance. Look at the picture.

1. What does the balance show about the two boxes of cookies?

_____

_____

Tina also brought juice to share equally with her group. But none of the glasses she brought were the same size. Before she poured the juice, Tina wanted to be sure each classmate had the same amount. For each classmate, she used a measuring cup and measured 1 cup. Then she poured the juice into a glass. She noticed that the level of the juice was different in all the glasses.

12-oz glass

15-oz glass

20-oz glass

2. Why was it a good idea that Tina measured the juice in a measuring cup

before pouring it into each glass? _____

_____

_____

_____

Harcourt

Use with page E21.

Name _____

Date _____

Distinguish Fact and Opinion

Write whether each sentence is a fact or an opinion.

1. The same volume of liquid may look different in different containers.

_____

2. Using measuring cups is the best way to measure liquids.

_____

3. Softballs are heavy.

_____

4. A golf ball has more mass than a Ping Pong ball.

_____

5. The dog weighs 8 kilograms (about 18 lb).

_____

6. When you cut an apple into halves, you still have the same amount of mass.

_____

7. Apples are the best fruit for snacking because they have a lot of mass.

_____

8. Measuring apples is easy if you know how to do it.

_____

9. A balance accurately measures mass.

_____

10. All scientists use balances.

_____

Harcourt

Name _____

Date _____

How Can Matter Be Measured?

Lesson Concept

Volume is the amount of space an object takes up. Mass is how much matter is in an object. Different objects can have the same volume but different masses.

Vocabulary

volume (E22)	**mass** (E24)

Put a check mark in front of the statement in each pair that agrees with what you have learned.

_____ **1.** The amount of space matter takes up is called mass.

_____ The amount of space matter takes up is called volume.

_____ **2.** You can tell how much mass an object has just by looking at it.

_____ You can measure an object to tell how much mass it has.

_____ **3.** Mass is the amount of liquid in an object.

_____ Mass is the amount of matter in an object.

_____ **4.** Air is a gas that cannot be seen and has no mass.

_____ Air and other gases have mass.

_____ **5.** Different kinds of matter can take up the same amount of space but have different masses.

_____ If different kinds of matter take up the same amount of space, they have the same mass.

Harcourt

Name _____

Date _____

Recognize Vocabulary

Match each term in Column A with its definition in Column B.

Column A

_____ **1.** It does not have a definite shape or a definite volume.

_____ **2.** They are the basic building blocks of matter.

_____ **3.** This is the process in which a liquid becomes a gas.

_____ **4.** This is the amount of space matter takes up.

_____ **5.** It is anything you can observe about an object by using your senses.

_____ **6.** All matter has volume and ____.

_____ **7.** It is anything that takes up space.

_____ **8.** It takes up a specific amount of space and has a definite shape.

_____ **9.** It has a volume that stays the same, but it can change its shape.

Column B

A mass

B volume

C evaporation

D solid

E matter

F atoms

G physical property

H liquid

I gas

Harcourt

Use with pages E4–E29.

Name _____

Date _____

Tell How to Check Volume

Informative Writing–How-to

Everyone on the soccer team was asked to bring two liters of water to the game. Each player brought the water in a different size and shape of container. No one brought a measuring cup, but one player brought the water in a 2-liter bottle. Write a set of steps for checking whether each player brought the right amount of water. Do not use a measuring cup. Use the outline below to plan your writing.

Step 1:

Step 2:

Step 3:

Step 4:

Harcourt

Chapter 2 • Graphic Organizer for Chapter Concepts

Changes in Matter

LESSON 1
PHYSICAL CHANGES

Ways Matter Can Change Physically and Still Be the Same Matter

1. _____

2. _____

3. _____

Ways To Physically Mix Matter

1. _____

2. _____

LESSON 2
CHEMICAL CHANGES

During a chemical change, _____.

Examples of Chemical Changes

1. _____

2. _____

How Chemical Changes Are Used

1. _____

2. _____

3. _____

Harcourt

🔍 **Investigate Log**

Separate a Mixture

Materials

4 clear plastic cups　　　**6 marbles**　　　**water**

steel paper clips　　　**rice**　　　**magnet**

measuring cup　　　**paper towels**　　　**funnel**

Activity Procedure

1 In one cup, make a mixture of marbles and water. Plan a way to separate the marbles from the water. Try it. **Record** your method and your results.

My method: _____

My results: _____

2 In another cup, make a mixture of marbles, paper clips, and rice. Plan a way to separate the mixture. Try it. **Record** your method and your results.

My method: _____

My results: _____

Harcourt

3 If your method doesn't work, plan a different way to separate the mixture. Try different methods until you find one that works. Try using the magnet. **Record** each method you try and your results.

My method: _____

My results: _____

4 In another cup, mix $\frac{1}{4}$ cup of rice with 1 cup of water. How could you separate the rice from the water? **Record** your ideas.

My ideas: _____

5 Make a filter with the paper towels and the funnel. **Predict** how this tool could be used to separate the mixture. Then use the filter to separate the mixture.

My prediction: _____

Draw Conclusions

1. When would it be easy to use only your hands to separate a mixture?

_____

_____

2. When might you need a tool to separate a mixture? _____

_____

_____

3. Scientists at Work Scientists often use charts to **record** the results of an investigation. How would setting up charts help you **plan and conduct an experiment**? _____

_____

_____

Investigate Further Make a mixture of sand and water. **Plan and conduct an experiment** to separate the mixture. Would a tool be useful? _____

Which tool would you use? _____

Harcourt

Name _____

Date _____

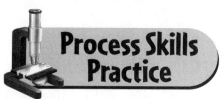
Plan and Conduct an Experiment

You plan and conduct an experiment to find the answer to a question or to solve a problem.

Think About Planning and Conducting an Experiment

Trey mistakenly dumped a large bag of flour into the kitchen rice container. He planned and conducted two experiments testing ways to separate the mixture. He recorded the results of his experiments.

Experiment #1 Made a small mixture of flour and rice in a jar. Picked the rice out, piece by piece. Result: Took too long. Was not a good method.	**Experiment #2** Made a small mixture of flour and rice in a jar. Used a strainer set over a bowl. Poured mixture into strainer. Result: Flour went through the strainer into bowl. Rice stayed in strainer. Good method for separating the mixture.

1. Why didn't the first experiment work? _____

_____

2. Why did Trey try two experiments before attempting to separate the

large mixture in his kitchen? _____

_____

3. What might have happened if he hadn't done the experiments?

_____

_____

Harcourt

Use with page E39.

Name _____

Date _____

Arrange Events in Sequence

The following sets of sentences are out of order. Rewrite the sentences in each set so that they are in the correct sequence.

Physical Changes in Matter

The sun melted Jane's ice cream.
Jane left the bowl of ice cream outside on a warm day.
The ice cream became liquid.
Jane placed a scoop of ice cream in a bowl.

_____

_____

_____

_____

The paint turned purple.
Lou wanted to make purple paint.
He stirred the two colors together.
Lou poured blue paint into red paint.

_____

_____

_____

_____

Use with page E43.

Harcourt

Name _____

Date _____

What Are Physical Changes?

Lesson Concept

Physical changes don't form new kinds of matter.

Vocabulary

physical changes (E40)   **mixture** (E41)   **solution** (E42)

Write the letter of the best answer on the lines.

1. In winter the pond water freezes. People skate on the ice. When the

   water freezes, _____.
   - **A** new matter is formed
   - **B** the matter becomes a mixture
   - **C** the matter is the same matter
   - **D** the matter becomes a solution

2. A young girl cut a sheet of paper into paper dolls. The paper has gone

   through a _____.
   - **A** physical change
   - **B** matter change
   - **C** state change

3. Emily poured raisins, apple slices, and cinnamon into a bowl. She stirred

   them together. The raisins, apple slices, and cinnamon are _____.
   - **A** a solution
   - **B** a mixture
   - **C** a condensation

4. A glass of lemonade was left out in the backyard. After a few days, only

   the sugar remained. What separated the solution? _____
   - **A** condensation
   - **B** evaporation
   - **C** precipitation

5. A solution is a kind of mixture that _____.
   - **A** cannot be eaten
   - **B** cannot freeze
   - **C** cannot be separated by hand

Harcourt

Use with page E43.

Chemical Changes

Materials

safety goggles

cookie sheet

large glass bowl

measuring cup

baking soda

vinegar

CAUTION ## Activity Procedure

1 CAUTION **Put on your safety goggles.**

2 Place the cookie sheet on the table. Place the bowl on the cookie sheet.

3 **Measure** $\frac{1}{4}$ cup of baking soda. Pour it into the bowl.

4 **Measure** $\frac{1}{4}$ cup of vinegar. Hold the cup with the vinegar in one hand. Use your other hand to fan some of the air from the cup toward your nose. Do not put your nose directly over the cup.

5 Pour the vinegar into the bowl.

6 **Observe** the matter in the bowl. **Record** what it looks like. Use the procedure from Step 4 to smell the matter in the bowl. Record what it smells like.

What it looks like: _____

_____

What it smells like: _____

_____

Harcourt

Name _____

Draw Conclusions

1. How is the material in the bowl like the baking soda and vinegar you

   started with? _____

   How is it different? _____

2. What can you **infer** about where the bubbles came from?

   _____

   _____

   _____

3. **Scientists at Work** Scientists **observe** changes. Then they **record** their
   observations. Describe the changes you observed in the bowl.

   _____

   _____

Investigate Further Mix warm water and a fresh packet of dry yeast.
Observe the mixture. **Record** what you see. What can you **infer** about the

changes you see? _____

   _____

   _____

Harcourt

Name _____

Date _____

Observe and Infer

You use your senses to observe the world around you. When you infer, you use your observations to form an opinion.

Think About Observing and Inferring

Tasha had some pennies that looked dull and were brown colored. She wanted to find out what the pennies looked like when they were new. She put on safety goggles. She put the pennies in a jar. Then she added $\frac{1}{4}$ cup of vinegar. She noticed the strong smell of the vinegar. She saw that the pennies were not fully covered, so she poured in more vinegar. After 15 minutes she looked in the jar. The pennies were now bright and shiny. They were copper colored just as they were when they were new. The vinegar was dark colored.

1. Why was it important for Tasha to wear safety goggles when she did the

   experiment? _____

2. What senses did Tasha use in this experiment, and how did she use them?

   _____

   _____

3. What observations did Tasha make about the pennies and the vinegar

   after the experiment was completed? _____

   _____

4. What can you infer about what changed the color of the pennies?

   _____

   _____

   _____

Harcourt

Use with page E45.

Name _____

Date _____

Summarize and Paraphrase a Selection

Chemical Changes at Home

Many kinds of chemical changes can occur in the home every day. A chemical change happens when you bake a cake. When someone eats the cake, chemical changes happen in the body. One occurs when saliva in the mouth mixes with the food. Some of the starches in the food are changed to sugar. The burning of fuel is a chemical change. A furnace may burn oil to heat a home. When wood is burned in the fireplace, a new kind of matter called ash is formed. Rusting is a chemical change. Iron nails that have been exposed to air and water can rust. Chemical changes called photosynthesis occur in plants when they make their own food.

1. What is the main idea of the paragraph?

_____

_____

_____

2. What are six examples that support the main idea?

_____

_____

_____

_____

_____

_____

Harcourt

Name _____

Date _____

What Are Chemical Changes?

Lesson Concept

Chemical changes cause new kinds of matter to form.

Vocabulary

chemical changes (E46)

Use a word from the list below to complete each of the following statements.

matter	physical	rusting

1. The kind of matter stays the same in _____ changes.

2. _____ is a chemical change that damages metal.

3. In a chemical change, the particles of matter change to form a new kind

of _____.

Answer the questions below.

1. Explain why burning wood is a chemical change.

_____

_____

2. What are some chemical changes that you notice

in your daily life? _____

_____

_____

_____

Use with page E49.

Recognize Vocabulary

Write the letter of the correct answer in the blank.

1. In a chemical change, two kinds of matter combine to form _____.

   A a different kind of matter   **B** a mixture

2. After a physical change, _____.

   A new matter is formed   **B** matter often looks different

3. A mixture is a substance that contains _____.

   A only one type of matter   **B** two or more types of matter

4. A solution is a mixture of _____.

   A different kinds of particles mixed together evenly   **B** some particles that are mixed together and some that stay apart

Put a check mark on the lines of the paragraphs that talk about chemical changes.

_____ **1.** The Sinclair family is celebrating Jacob Sinclair's fifth birthday with a camping trip. Before they go, Jacob's mother makes cupcakes. She mixes together flour, milk, eggs, butter, and chocolate. She puts the cupcakes in the oven to bake. When they are done, she frosts them.

_____ **2.** Next, Mrs. Sinclair makes a piñata. She cuts up paper and soaks the paper in glue. Then she forms the paper into the shape of a cow. She stuffs the piñata with candy.

_____ **3.** At the campsite that night, the Sinclair family builds a fire in the fire pit. First, the wooden logs go in, and then the fire is lighted. The logs burn brightly, smoke rises in the air, and ashes fall from the burned wood.

_____ **4.** The next morning the family gets ready to go home. They gather up all the trash. They throw the food scraps into a special container and mix them all together. Then they get in the car to drive home.

Harcourt

Name _____

Date _____

Compare Combinations

Informative Writing—Compare and Contrast

Write a paragraph about mixtures and solutions. Give an example of each of these combinations of matter. Tell how they are alike and how they are different. Use the Venn diagram below to help you plan your writing.

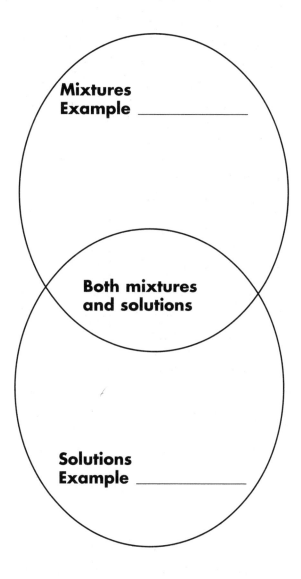

Mixtures
Example _____

Both mixtures and solutions

Solutions
Example _____

Harcourt

Name _____ Date _____

Energy

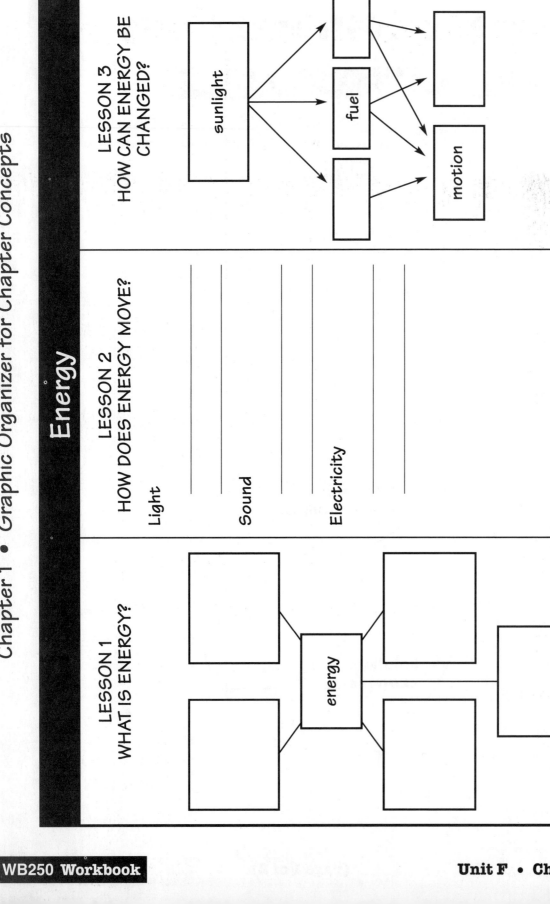

LESSON 1
WHAT IS ENERGY?

energy

LESSON 2
HOW DOES ENERGY MOVE?

Light _____

Sound _____

Electricity _____

LESSON 3
HOW CAN ENERGY BE CHANGED?

sunlight

fuel

motion

Twisting Up Energy

Materials

goggles

2 clothespins

1 rubber band

Activity Procedure

1 **CAUTION** Put on safety goggles to protect your eyes in case a clothespin pops loose.

2 Attach the rubber band to each clothespin. Work with a partner to twist the rubber band between the clothespins.

3 When you have finished, the rubber band should be twisted and curled up.

4 Holding the clothespins tightly, lay them on the table and **hypothesize** what will happen to them when you let them go. **Communicate** your hypothesis to your partner.

5 **Observe** what happens to the clothespins when you let them go. Then do the investigation again, this time twisting the pins more tightly than you did before. **Compare** what the clothespins did the first time with what they did the second time.

Harcourt

Draw Conclusions

1. Describe what happened each time you put the clothespins on the table and let go of them. How did your hypothesis compare to the actual

results? _____

_____

_____

2. Where did the energy to move the clothespins come from?

_____

_____

_____

3. **Scientists at Work** Scientists **conduct simple experiments** to learn more about how things work. What did you learn about energy and

twisted rubber bands from your investigation? _____

_____

_____

_____

Investigate Further **Observe** what happens to a third clothespin that you twist around the other two with a second rubber band.

_____

_____

_____

Harcourt

Name _____

Date _____

Hypothesize

When you hypothesize before conducting a simple investigation, you are explaining what you think will happen. Your hypothesis can be based on things you have observed, things you already know to be true, or things you have learned from earlier investigations.

Think About Hypothesizing

Harry has a windup toy. He noticed that when he winds it up six twists, it hops twelve times, on average. But when he winds it up three twists, it hops an average of six times. He developed a hypothesis: the toy will always hop twice the number of twists.

1. Where does the windup toy gets its energy? _____

_____

2. How can Harry test his hypothesis? _____

_____

3. How should Harry record his tests? _____

_____

_____

4. What if the results of his tests do not prove his hypothesis? What can he

do? _____

_____

_____

5. If Harry looked inside the toy, what do you think he would find that

stores the energy? _____

_____

Name _____

Date _____

Reading Skills Practice

Compare and Contrast

Complete the chart below to compare how energy is used.

Two Things That Use or Produce Energy	How Are These Things Alike?	How Are These Things Different?
plants animals		
electric heater fireplace		
cars people		
wood battery		
food fossil fuel		

Harcourt

Name _____

Date _____

What Is Energy?

Lesson Concept

Energy is the ability to move something. All living things and machines need energy to function. Energy comes mainly from the sun, and can be found in many different forms. It can be stored and used later.

Vocabulary

energy (F6)   **electricity** (F7)   **fossil fuel** (F8)

potential energy (F6)   **kinetic energy** (F7)

Draw a line from each living thing or object in the left column to the source of the energy it uses in the right column.

1.

2.

3.

4.

5.

A

B

C

D

E

Harcourt

Waves of Energy

Materials

**rope
about 6 feet long**

**coiled
spring toy**

Activity Procedure

1 Do this investigation with a partner. Hold one end of the rope while your partner holds the other. Stand so that the rope hangs loosely between you.

2 While your partner holds his or her end of the rope still, move your end gently up and down. Now move the rope faster. **Compare** what the rope looked like before with what it looks like now.

3 Now take the coiled spring toy and place it on a table or on the floor. Hold one end, and have your partner hold the other.

4 Ask your partner to hold the end still as you quickly push your end of the toy in about 4 inches. Now push and pull your end backward and forward. **Observe** what happens to the coils.

5 Draw and label a diagram explaining what happened to the rope when you moved one end. Make another diagram showing what happened to the coiled spring toy when you pushed one end in.

Harcourt

Name _____

Investigate Log

Draw Conclusions

1. What happened to the rope when you moved one end up and down? How did it move? What happened when you moved it faster?

_____

_____

_____

_____

2. What happened when you pushed your end of the coiled spring toy toward your partner? What happened when you moved it back and

forth? _____

_____

_____

_____

3. Scientists at Work When things in nature can't be seen, scientists **use models** to see how they work. They then **communicate** what they learn. How did your diagram help you to communicate what you learned about

how energy moves as waves? _____

_____

_____

_____

Harcourt

Name _____

Date _____

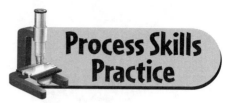

Use Models and Communicate

You can use objects that you can see to model things that you cannot see. Then you can draw and label diagrams to communicate what you have learned. Models can include maps, pictures and diagrams, three-dimensional representations, and computer simulations.

Think About Using Models

We cannot see sounds, but if we observe carefully, we can see and feel the vibrations that make sounds happen. Observe the three pictures below.

1. What would you hear if you plucked the rubber band with your finger?

_____

2. How would the rubber band look while you were hearing the sound?

_____

3. If you placed a vibrating tuning fork into a bowl of water, what would you see?

_____

_____

4. Do sound waves travel through water?

_____

5. If you cover a comb with a piece of wax paper and then hum with your lips touching the wax paper, what would you feel?

_____

Harcourt

Use with page F15.

Name _____

Date _____

Use Prefixes and Suffixes to Determine Word Meaning

A word's meaning can be changed by adding a prefix or a suffix to the root word. Below is a list of root words and their definitions. Choose one prefix or one suffix from the box, and write the new word. Then write the definition of the new word.

prefixes	suffixes
re- un- pre-	-ing -tion -ity -ian

1. *move:* to change position from one point to another

prefix or suffix added: _____

new word: _____

definition: _____

2. *vent:* to allow something to be released through an opening

prefix or suffix added: _____

new word: _____

definition: _____

3. *electric:* made of or powered by electricity

prefix or suffix added: _____

new word: _____

definition: _____

4. *vibrate:* move back and forth very quickly

prefix or suffix added: _____

new word: _____

definition: _____

Harcourt

How Does Energy Move?

Lesson Concept

Energy can move in many different ways. Light energy moves as up-and-down waves. Sound energy moves as back-and-forth waves. Electricity moves from batteries to other objects. Thermal energy moves as heat and is transferred by touching or by radiation.

Vocabulary

vibrate (F19)   **circuit** (F20)

Read the sentence for clues to unscramble the term that belongs in the blank. Then rewrite the unscrambled term in the blank.

1. Sound energy and light move in _____. **VSEAW**

2. Light travels _____ than sound. **STREAF**

3. When you rub your hands together to get them warm, you make

   _____ energy. **MARETLH**

4. In a circuit, energy travels from the _____ through the wires to the bulb. **RABYTET**

5. _____ vibrations can travel through liquids, solids, and gases. **ONDSU**

6. When you feel the thermal energy of hot cocoa in a cup, you are feeling

   _____. **AETH**

7. Thermal energy that moves without touching anything is called

   _____. **AORIDINAT**

8. Fuel is a form of _____ energy. **SEDTOR**

Harcourt

Name _____

Date _____

Lighting a Bulb

Materials

masking tape

D-cell battery

2 pieces of
insulated electrical wire

miniature light bulb

Activity Procedure

1. Use a piece of masking tape to tape the battery to your desk. This way, it won't roll around.

2. As your partner holds the light bulb a few inches away from the battery, use the wires to connect the ends of the battery with the base of the bulb.

3. Now switch the wires. Do you **observe** any changes?

4. Try to make the bulb light by touching the wires to the glass part of the bulb. Can you make it light?

5. Can you make the bulb light by touching the wires to the sides of the battery?

Harcourt

Name _____

Investigate Log

Draw Conclusions

1. What happened when you connected the ends of the battery to the base of the light bulb by using the wires? _____
   _____

2. What happened when you switched the wires? _____
   _____

3. Could you make the bulb light by touching the wires to the glass part of the bulb? Did the bulb light when you touched the wires to the sides of the battery? _____

4. **Scientists at Work** Scientists know that the results of experiments don't often turn out exactly the same every time. This can be caused by differences in materials or differences in procedure. How could you change the materials in this investigation to see if the results would change?

   MEFRODP+I/L:

Investigate Further Plan and conduct a simple investigation to find out if you can make the bulb light by using something other than wires to connect the battery and the bulb. **Control variables** by using the same battery and bulb for each trial.

_____

_____

_____

_____

Harcourt

Name _____

Date _____

Experiment and Draw Conclusions

When you do an experiment, you make a hypothesis. Then you gather data to test your hypothesis. You can observe and see evidence that helps you draw conclusions about why your hypothesis was—or was not—correct.

Think About Experimenting

In a circuit like the one in Diagram A, the light bulb will light. What do you think will happen if you add another battery to the circuit as in Diagram B?

Diagram A   **Diagram B**

1. Do you think the light bulb will light in the circuit shown in Diagram B?

_____

2. Do you think the light would be brighter in Diagram B? Explain your

answer. _____

_____

3. What do you think would happen if you added two more batteries to the

circuit? _____

_____

Name _____

Date _____

Use Reference Sources

Use reference sources such as books, newspapers, magazines, or the Internet to write a paragraph or fact sheet about one of the topics below. List your reference sources and write your paragraph on this sheet.

Topics

1. Ways to Conserve Energy in the Home

2. How Greenhouses Help Plants Grow

3. How Windmills Are Used

4. How Solar Panels Work to Help Heat Homes

Your topic: _____

Reference sources used: _____

_____

_____

_____

_____

_____

_____

_____

_____

Harcourt

How Can Energy Be Changed?

Lesson Concept

Energy can change forms. Sunlight can become food, fuel, or electricity. Electricity can become other kinds of energy, such as light, heat, and motion. Food and fuel can become motion and heat.

Vocabulary

waste heat (F26)

Number these pictures in the correct sequence to show how energy is converted into different forms.

_____

_____

_____

_____

Harcourt

Recognize Vocabulary

In the space provided, write the letter of the term in column B that
best fits the definition in column A. Use each term only once.

Column A

_____ 1. The ability to cause change

_____ 2. Where the energy in food comes from

_____ 3. A form of energy that travels through
space as up-and-down waves

_____ 4. A form of energy that travels through
material as back-and-forth waves

_____ 5. The type of energy found in food and fuel

_____ 6. The kind of energy that powers your
refrigerator and your hair dryer

_____ 7. The path electricity follows

_____ 8. Fuel formed from organisms that lived
millions of years ago

Column B

A electricity

B potential energy

C energy

D waste heat

E sound

F fossil fuel

G vibrate

H light

I circuit

J the sun

K kinetic energy

Choose two of the vocabulary terms from column B. Then, using
your own words, write a sentence that uses each term correctly.

_____

_____

_____

_____

Harcourt

Name _____

Date _____

Tell a Story About Energy

Narrative Writing—Story

Tell the story of the gasoline that your family car or school bus runs on. Tell where it came from and what happened to the original matter through each step. Complete the sentences in the outline below to help you plan your writing.

> Long ago, dinosaurs . . .

⬇

> Decayed matter from dead dinosaurs . . .

⬇

> Over time, the decayed matter was changed into . . .

⬇

> Oil and gas companies dug wells in the ground to get . . .

⬇

> In the car or bus engine, the gasoline . . .

Harcourt

Chapter 2 • Graphic Organizer for Chapter Concepts

Heat

LESSON 1
HEAT

What Is Heat?

_____

How to Make Things Hot

1. _____

2. _____

3. _____

Three Ways We Use Heat

1. _____

2. _____

3. _____

LESSON 2
THERMAL ENERGY
ON THE MOVE

Ways Thermal Energy Can Move

1. _____

2. _____

3. _____

Moving Through Materials

1. moves easily through a _____

2. can't move easily through an _____

LESSON 3
TEMPERATURE

How Thermal Energy Is Measured

_____

**How Humans Control
Thermal Energy**

1. _____

2. _____

Harcourt

Rubbing Objects Together

Materials

metal button   **small piece of wool**   **penny**   **sheet of paper**

Activity Procedure

1 Hold your bare hands together, palms touching. Do your hands feel cold, hot, sticky, or damp? **Record** what you **observe**.

2 Make a **hypothesis**. What would you feel if you rubbed your hands together? **Record** your hypothesis.

3 Now rub your palms together very fast for about ten seconds. **Record** what you **observe**.

4 What might you feel if you rubbed the button with the wool? The penny with paper? Form a **hypothesis** for each test. **Record** each one.

5 Rub the button with the wool for about ten seconds. Touch the button. Touch the wool. **Record** what you **observe**.

6 Then rub the penny with the paper for about ten seconds. Touch the penny. Touch the paper. **Record** what you **observe**.

Harcourt

Name _____

Investigate Log

Draw Conclusions

1. What changes did you **observe**? What actions did you perform that caused the changes you observed? _____

_____

_____

2. Were your **hypotheses** correct? If not, how could you change them based on what you learned? _____

_____

_____

3. **Scientists at Work** Scientists use their knowledge and experiences to help them **hypothesize**. What knowledge and experiences did you use in this investigation to help you hypothesize? _____

_____

_____

Harcourt

Name _____

Date _____

Hypothesize

When you hypothesize, you say what you think will happen if something else happens.

Think About Hypothesizing

Lisa went to science class and read these two statements on the board:

1. Bend a piece of wire back and forth five or six times. After you bend it, you will notice that the bend in the wire feels cool.

2. Bend a piece of wire back and forth five or six times. After you bend it, you will notice that the bend in the wire feels warm.

One of the statements was wrong. To find out which hypothesis was wrong, Lisa did an experiment: She took a piece of stiff wire about 30 centimeters (12 in.) long. She felt the wire. It felt cool. She bent the wire back and forth about five or six times. Then she felt the bend in the wire. The bend in the wire felt warm.

1. Draw a line under the first hypothesis. What does it state about the bend

in the wire? _____

_____

2. Draw a line under the second hypothesis. What does it state about the

bend in the wire? _____

_____

3. Which hypothesis is correct? Why is it correct? _____

_____

_____

Harcourt

Name _____

Date _____

Arrange Events in Sequence

Rewrite the following words and phrases so they show the movement of thermal energy in order.

1. cup

   pot   _____

   soup

   burner

   mouth

2. hot charcoal

   hamburger   _____

   lit match

   grill

3. warmed hands

   rubbing together   _____

   bare hands   _____

4. hot air

   wet clothes   _____

   dry clothes

5. mittens

   warm hands inside mittens   _____

   cold hands wearing mittens _____

   campfire

Harcourt

Concept Review

What Is Heat?

Lesson Concept

Energy is the ability to cause matter to change. Thermal energy is the energy of the movement of the particles inside matter. Thermal energy that moves from one thing to another is called heat.

Vocabulary

thermal energy (F39)　　　**heat** (F40)　　　**friction** (F41)

As you read the summary, fill in each blank with one of the vocabulary terms from above.

_____ is the force between two moving objects that keeps the objects from moving freely. There are different kinds of energy.

All kinds of energy cause change. _____ is the kind of energy that moves particles in matter, and it is felt as

_____. Heat is the movement of thermal energy from one place to another. There are a number of ways to produce thermal energy. Rubbing things together, burning things, and mixing chemicals are three ways to produce thermal energy. Thermal energy is used in everyday life for things such as cooking and keeping people warm.

Underline the correct answer.

1. What are the particles in solids, liquids, and gases doing all the time?

　A dissolving　　**B** reacting　　**C** increasing　　**D** moving

Answer each question with one or more complete sentences.

2. Describe what happens to thermal energy when you touch a hot cup

　of cocoa. _____

3. Describe what happens to thermal energy when you touch a cold glass

　of juice. _____

Name _____

Date _____

What Gets Hot

Materials

wooden spoon

plastic spoon

metal spoon

3 foam cups

water

ceramic mug

plastic cup with handle

metal cup with handle

CAUTION ## Activity Procedure

1 Use the chart below to **record** your **observations**.

2 Touch the three spoons. Are they hot or cold? **Record** what you **observe**.

3 **CAUTION** **Be careful with hot water. It can burn you.** Fill three foam cups with hot tap water. Set them on the table in front of you. Put one spoon in each cup. Wait one minute.

4 Gently touch each spoon. Which one is hottest? **Record** how hot each spoon is. Use words like *cool, warm,* or *hot.*

5 Next, fill each cup with hot tap water. Wait one minute. Then gently touch the handle of each cup. Which one is hottest?

6 Use the words you wrote in Step 4 to **record** how hot each cup handle is.

Spoons			Cups		
Wooden	Plastic	Metal	Ceramic	Plastic	Metal

Harcourt

Name _____

Draw Conclusions

1. Study your Spoons chart. Did all the spoons get hot? Which spoon got

the hottest? _____

_____

_____

_____

2. Look at both charts. Which material got hot in both experiments?
How did the plastic items change in the hot water?

_____

_____

_____

_____

3. Scientists at Work As they test their ideas, scientists may change their
experiments in small ways. Suppose you want to see if wood always stays
cool when it is placed near heat. What kinds of wooden objects could you

use in your experiment? _____

_____

_____

Harcourt

Name _____

Date _____

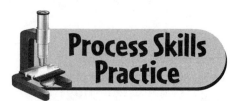

Experiment

You do an experiment to find out new information. An experiment is a kind of test.

Think About Experimenting

During a camping trip, the boys and girls did two experiments. First, they used a long, wooden stick to stir the potatoes that were roasting in the fire. Then, they used a long metal spoon. They found that the wooden stick stayed cool. The long, metal spoon heated up. For their second experiment, they took the cooked potatoes out of the fire. They wrapped one in foil and one in a piece of wool. They felt each of the potatoes several different times. They were surprised to learn that the wool kept the potato warm for a longer time than the foil did.

1. What information do you think the boys and girls were trying to gather when they did the experiment with the wooden stick and the metal

   spoon? _____

   _____

2. What did they learn from the experiment? _____

   _____.

3. What information do you think they were trying to gather when they did

   the experiment with the potatoes? _____

   _____

4. What did they learn from that experiment? _____

   _____

5. Why do you think the boys and girls were surprised at the information

   they gathered? _____

   _____

   _____

Harcourt

Use with page F45.

Name _____

Date _____

Summarize and Paraphrase a Selection

Thermal Heat Moving Through Things

A conductor allows thermal energy to move easily from one thing to another. Many things are made from materials that are good conductors. Cooking pots and pans are usually made of metal because metal allows thermal energy to move quickly to the food that is being heated. People often use wooden spoons to stir hot liquids on the stove because a metal spoon would heat up quickly and be too hot to handle.

An insulator, on the other hand, does not let thermal energy move easily through it. People use these materials to insulate their homes. In the winter, insulation keeps heat from easily leaving the home. In the summer, insulation also helps keep warm air from entering the house. Mittens are good insulators because they keep body heat from easily leaving the inside of the mitten.

Write an outline for the above paragraphs.

I. _____

_____

    A. _____

    B. _____

II. _____

    A. _____

    B. _____

_____

    C. _____

Harcourt

Concept Review

How Does Thermal Energy Move?

Lesson Concept

Thermal energy can move when objects touch and particles bump into each other. It can move from one place to another in moving liquids or gases. Thermal energy from the sun moves by radiation.

Vocabulary		
	conduction (F46)	**conductor** (F47)
insulator (F47)	**convection** (F48)	**radiation** (F48)

As you read the summary, fill in each blank with one of the vocabulary terms from above. Then answer the questions that follow.

A _____ lets thermal energy travel easily. An

_____ is a material in which thermal energy doesn't move easily. The particles in heated liquids and gases can move from one place to another. Thermal energy that moves without touching anything, like thermal energy from the sun, moves by radiation.

1. Jessica is making scrambled eggs in a frying pan for breakfast. Do the

eggs cook by convection or conduction? _____

2. _____ is the type of movement resulting from the way thermal energy moves in liquids and gases.

3. Thermal energy that moves without touching anything is called

_____ .

Harcourt

Measuring Temperature

Materials

| 2 cups | thermometer | water |

CAUTION Activity Procedure

1 Use the chart below.

2 **CAUTION** **Be careful with hot water. It can burn you.** Fill one of the cups with cold tap water. Fill the other with hot tap water.

3 Put the thermometer into the cup of cold water. **Observe** what happens to the liquid in the thermometer. On your chart, **record** the temperature.

4 Put the thermometer into the cup of hot water. **Observe** what happens to the liquid in the thermometer. On your chart, **record** the temperature.

5 Put the thermometer back into the cup of cold water. **Observe** what happens to the liquid in the thermometer. On your chart, **record** the temperature.

6 Wait one minute. Put the thermometer back into the cup of hot water. **Observe** what happens to the liquid in the thermometer. On your chart, **record** the temperature.

Water	Temperature
Cold water, Step 3	
Hot water, Step 4	
Cold water, Step 5	
Hot water, Step 6	

Harcourt

Name _____

Draw Conclusions

1. What happened to the liquid inside the thermometer each time you put the thermometer in the hot water? What happened when you put it in the cold water? _____

_____

_____

2. Was the temperature of the hot water the same both times you **measured** it? What do you think caused you to get the measurements you got?

_____

_____

3. Scientists at Work Scientists **measure** carefully. Write directions for how to measure temperature by using a thermometer. _____

_____

_____

Harcourt

Name _____

Date _____

Measure

Measuring is a way to observe things accurately. You can record the measurements you observe.

Think About Measuring

Christina bought a Christmas Cactus [*Schlumbergera*]. She learned that if she wanted the plant to bloom at Christmas, she would need to keep the plant where night temperatures would be between 10°C and 12°C (50° F and 55° F), beginning in November. Christina decided to measure the temperature in several areas in the house for three nights. Christina observed and recorded the temperatures at 8:00 P.M. each night. Her mother observed and recorded the temperatures at 11:00 P.M. After looking at the recorded temperatures, Christina chose the basement as the place to keep her plant.

		Basement Temp.	Kitchen Temp.	Living Room Temp.
Monday	8:00 P.M.	53°	68°	70°
	11:00 P.M.	51°	63°	68°
Tuesday	8:00 P.M.	55°	70°	70°
	11:00 P.M.	52°	65°	67°
Wednesday	8:00 P.M.	54°	67°	69°
	11:00 P.M.	50°	62°	66°

1. Why is it better to measure the temperature than to guess?

_____

_____

_____

2. Which of the areas where they were measuring temperature was the warmest at night in Christina's house? How do you know?

_____

Harcourt

Name _____

Date _____

Identify Cause and Effect

Underline the causes and circle the effects in the sentences below.

1. In thermometers the temperature of the air outside a glass tube causes the liquid inside the tube to move up or down.

2. Inside a thermometer the liquid expands when it is warm and travels up the tube.

3. When the liquid cools, the particles get closer together and sink down the tube.

4. When water reaches 0°C (32°F), it freezes.

5. When water reaches 100°C (212°F), it boils.

6. Lead melts when its temperature reaches 327°C (620°F).

7. When it gets cold in the winter, animals' fur becomes thicker.

8. Dressing lightly in hot weather helps people stay cool.

9. Adjusting a thermostat helps control the temperature inside a building.

10. A person with a fever has an increase in body temperature.

Name _____

Date _____

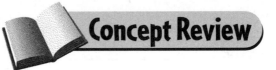
Concept Review

How Is Temperature Measured?

Lesson Concept

Temperature can be measured with a thermometer. People control heat by wearing clothing and by using thermostats.

Vocabulary

thermometer (F52)

Underline the correct answer.

1. A thermometer is a tool used to measure _____.

  A how hot or cold something is　**B** how big something is　**C** how fast something is

2. In a liquid thermometer, _____ makes the liquid inside expand and move up the tube.

  A thermal energy　**B** cold air　**C** controlling heat

3. The liquid in a thermometer moves up the tube when it gets hot because _____.

  A it needs less space　**B** its particles don't move as fast　**C** it needs more space

4. When the liquid in a thermometer sinks down in the tube, it means that _____.

  A the particles are not moving as fast　**B** the temperature is rising　**C** the liquid is getting warmer

5. A dial thermometer uses a _____ instead of a liquid.

  A scale　**B** metal coil　**C** tube

6. One way to control heat inside a building is by using a _____.

  A thermometer　**B** Fahrenheit scale　**C** thermostat

Harcourt

Use with page F55.

Recognize Vocabulary

Underline the correct meaning for each word.

1. friction

   A conduction

   B convection

   C radiation

2. thermal energy

   A the energy of particles moving in matter

   B the way things move

   C the act of ice melting

3. heat

   A the energy of movement of matter

   B a particle that begins to burn

   C the movement of thermal energy from one place to another

4. conductor

   A a material in which thermal energy doesn't move easily

   B a material in which thermal energy moves easily

   C a way to keep particles from moving

5. insulator

   A something that moves thermal energy from one object to another

   B a material in which thermal energy can't move easily

   C a material that conducts radiation

6. thermometer

   A a tool used to measure how hot or cold something is

   B a tool used to measure whether or not a material is a good conductor

   C a tool used to measure particles in matter

Harcourt

Name _____

Date _____

Write a Business Letter

Persuasive Writing–Request

Use reference sources to find the address of a nursery, recycling center, or county agricultural board near you. Write a letter requesting information on setting up and maintaining a home compost heap. Use the letter format below to help you plan your writing. Share what you learn with your class.

Heading:

Inside Address:

Greeting:

Body of letter:

Hint: Remember to thank the person you are writing to for his or her time and assistance.

Closing:

Signature:

Harcourt

Chapter 3 • Graphic Organizer for Chapter Concepts

Forces and Motion

LESSON 3
SIMPLE MACHINES

What Are Simple Machines?

_____

_____

The Six Simple Machines

1. _____

2. _____

3. _____

4. _____

5. _____

6. _____

LESSON 2
WORK

What Is Work?

_____

_____

These Things Are Work

1. _____

2. _____

3. _____

These Things Are NOT Work

1. _____

2. _____

3. _____

LESSON 1
MOTION

What Causes Motion?

_____

What Is Motion?

_____

_____

How Forces and Motion Interact

1. a force must be applied in
   order to get _____

_____

2. not all forces cause _____

_____

How fast something moves is its _____.

The force that pulls us to Earth is

_____.

Harcourt

Measuring Pushes and Pulls

Materials

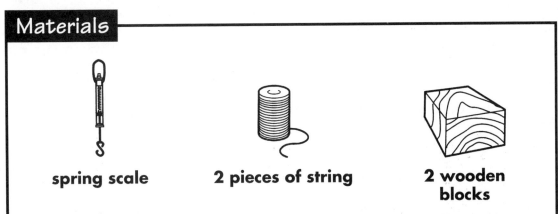

spring scale   2 pieces of string   2 wooden blocks

Activity Procedure

1 Work with a partner. One of you should hold one end of the spring scale while the other gently pulls on the hook. Read the number on the scale. The number is in newtons. Newtons measure pushes and pulls. **Record** the number.

2 Tie one piece of string around one of the wooden blocks. Tie the other end of the string to the hook on the scale.

3 Begin to pull on the spring scale. Pull as hard as you can without making the block move. **Record** the number on the scale.

4 Now pull hard enough to make the block move. **Record** the number on the scale. Carefully pull the block across the room. Watch the scale. Make sure the number doesn't change as you pull.

5 Repeat Step 4. This time, pull so that the number on the scale changes. **Record** your observations.

6 Tie the second wooden block to the first one. Repeat Steps 3 through 5. **Record** your observations.

Harcourt

Name _____

Draw Conclusions

1. How many newtons did it take to pull on the block without moving it? How many newtons did you use to move the block in Step 4?

_____

_____

_____

_____

2. How did you pull differently in Steps 4 and 5? _____

_____

_____

_____

_____

3. How did your results change when you added the second block?

_____

_____

4. **Scientists at Work** Scientists make charts to help them **interpret data.** Make a chart to organize the data you collected in this investigation.

_____

Harcourt

Name _____

Date _____

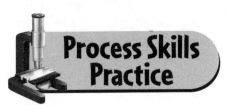

Gather and Interpret Data

You can gather and interpret data for experiments. You can record your data.

Think About Gathering and Interpreting Data

Mark put a small stone in a cloth bag. Then he tied the bag to a spring scale and let it hang down. The scale measured 2 newtons pulling the stone down. In a second test, Mark added another stone to the bag. He estimated that the scale would now measure 3 newtons pulling the stone down. But the measurement was 4 newtons. As a third test, Mark took out both stones and put a smaller one in the bag. This time the scale measured only 1 newton.

1. Arranging data in a table can make it easier to interpret. Fill out the following table.

	First Test	Second Test	Third Test
Number or size of stones			
Newtons	2	3	1

2. How many newtons pulled the stone down the first time? _____

3. In which test did the scale measure the most newtons? _____

4. Mark estimated the number of newtons for his second test. Then he measured. Why was it a good idea for him to measure? _____

_____

5. What do you think Mark learned from his experiments? _____

_____

_____

Harcourt

Use with page F65.

Name _____

Date _____

Identify Cause and Effect

The Games

The students in Mrs. Smith's class joined other students for an outdoor activity day at school. In the peanut race, Amanda had to push a peanut across the floor using her nose! The peanut moved very slowly. In the wheelbarrow race, John held Luis by his legs and pushed him forward toward the finish line. John accidentally pushed too hard, and Luis fell over. They both laughed. In another game, a group of students gathered in a circle and shot marbles. Samantha used her large marble to hit a smaller one, and the small marble shot across the circle. Samantha won for shooting her marble the farthest. The final game of the day was a large game of bumper ball. All the students sat in a circle. Each time that the cage ball came to a student, that student used his or her feet to bump the ball across the circle. It was a fun day.

What are some causes and effects in this selection? Finish the chart below.

Cause	Effect

Harcourt

How Do Forces Cause Motion?

Lesson Concept

Every motion is started and stopped by a force.

Vocabulary

force (F66)	**motion** (F67)	**speed** (F69)
gravity (F70)	**weight** (F70)	

Underline the correct answer.

1. You see a flock of birds flying across the sky. You know that the motion of the birds was begun by ____.

    A a force **B** gravity **C** a change in position **D** speed

2. Gravity is a ____.

    A lifting force **B** squeezing force **C** pushing force **D** pulling force

3. The measurement of the pull of Earth's gravity on an object is ____.

    A length **B** mass **C** weight **D** force

4. If you are comparing how fast two objects are moving over a certain distance, you are comparing their ____.

    A gravity **B** force **C** speed **D** mass

5. To stop something from moving, you have to apply ____.

    A balance **B** force **C** speed **D** weight

6. A change in position is called ____.

    A speed **B** weight **C** motion **D** mass

Name _____

Date _____

Investigate Log

Measuring Work

Materials

mug   spring scale   meterstick   string

shoe with laces   hat   stapler

Activity Procedure

1 Use the table on the next page.

2 Hook the mug onto the spring scale. Work with a partner. One of you should hold the meterstick on the table, with the 1-cm mark toward the bottom. The other person should rest the mug on the table next to the meterstick.

3 Gently lift the scale, and pull the mug off the table. Keep the scale and the mug next to the meterstick. **Record** the height you lifted the mug.

4 Read the number of newtons on the spring scale. **Record** the number.

5 Multiply the number of newtons you used times the distance you moved the mug. This is the amount of work that was done. **Record** this number in your table under the heading *Work*.

6 Repeat Steps 2 through 5, using each of the other objects. You may need to use the string to attach the objects to the spring scale. Lift each object the same distance you lifted the mug.

Harcourt

Name _____

Distance × Force = Work			
Object	**Distance (centimeters)**	**Force (newtons)**	**Work (newton-centimeters)**

Draw Conclusions

1. Which object took the most force to lift? Which object took the least

force to lift? _____

2. Describe the math you did in the table. _____

_____

_____

_____

3. In this investigation one of the measurements was kept the same.

Which one was it? _____

4. **Scientists at Work** Scientists **infer** from data. Look at the data you

collected. Infer how work is related to force. _____

_____

Harcourt

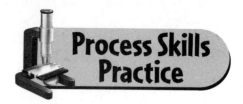

Infer

You can make an inference from data you collect when you do an experiment.

Think About Inferring

Using a spring scale and a string as shown below, Greg pulled a book across the top of a desk. It took a pulling force of 1 newton to move the book. Greg noticed there was a sheet of notebook paper under the book. He removed the sheet of notebook paper and tried again. This time it took 2 newtons to pull the book. Greg put the book on a sheet of construction paper. This time it took 3 newtons. Greg made the following table.

Force Needed to Move the Book	Surface
2 newtons	desk
1 newton	notebook paper
3 newtons	construction paper

1. What was different about the surfaces beneath the book? _____

_____

_____

2. Which surface made the book easier to move? Why do you think this is so?

_____

_____

3. What can you infer from this experiment about the work you need

to do to move something over a surface? Explain. _____

_____

_____

Harcourt

Name _____

Date _____

Reading Skills Practice

Arrange Events in Sequence

Rewrite the sentences so that they are in order. Look for clue words such as *first, then, next, after,* and *last* to help you.

Next, Dale began to push large amounts of snow with the shovel.

First, Dale put on his hat and gloves.

Finally, after one hour, Dale had cleared all the snow from the driveway.

Then, Dale chose a shovel from the garage.

_____

_____

_____

_____

Write a paragraph that describes how a man moved a wagonload of dirt from his front yard to his garden. Use clue words such as *first, then, next, after,* and *last.*

_____

_____

_____

_____

_____

Harcourt

Name _____

Date _____

What Is Work?

Lesson Concept

In science, work is done when a force moves an object.

Vocabulary

work (F74)

Answer each question with one or more complete sentences.

1. Jack worked very hard trying to push the piano in his living room. But the piano didn't move. Would a scientist say that Jack had done some

work? Explain why or why not. _____

_____

2. Jack's older sister helped him. They moved the piano to the other side of the living room. Would a scientist say that Jack and his sister had done

some work? Explain why or why not. _____

_____

_____

3. Emily used 60 newtons to lift her baby sister 1 meter in the air.

How could you figure out the amount of work done? _____

_____

4. How much work did Emily do? _____

Harcourt

Name _____

Date _____

Moving Up

Materials

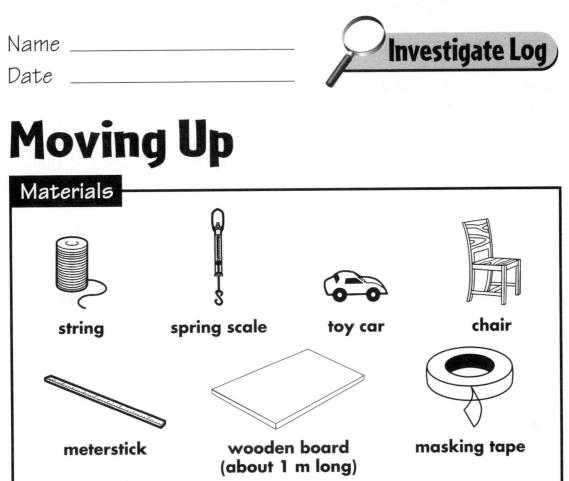

string spring scale toy car chair

meterstick wooden board (about 1 m long) masking tape

Activity Procedure

1. Using the string, attach the spring scale to the toy car. With the spring scale, slowly lift until the bottom of the car is at the same level as the seat of the chair. Read the spring scale, and **record** the number.

2. Use the meterstick to **measure** how high you lifted the car. **Record** this number, too.

3. Prop up one end of the board on the seat of the chair. Tape the board to the floor so the board does not move.

4. Now place the toy car at the bottom of the board. Slowly pull the car to the top of the board at a steady rate. As you pull, read the force on the spring scale. **Record** it.

5. **Measure** the distance you pulled the car up the board. **Record** it.

Name _____

Draw Conclusions

1. Multiply the force you **measured** by the distance you moved the toy car. How much work did you do without the board? How much work did you do with the board? _____

_____

_____

2. **Compare** the force used without the board to the force used with the board. Which method used less force? _____

_____

3. **Compare** the distance the car moved each time. Which method used less distance? _____

4. **Scientists at Work** Scientists often **compare** their data. Compare your answers to Question 1 to the answers of your classmates. What did you find out? _____

_____

_____

Investigate Further Repeat the activity using boards of several different lengths. **Record** the results. Did you use less force with longer boards or shorter ones?

Harcourt

Name _____

Date _____

Compare

When you compare, you look at two or more events to see how they are alike and how they are different.

Think About Comparing

Andre was visiting his Uncle Arthur in West Virginia. Behind his uncle's house was the steepest hill Andre had ever seen. He decided to climb it. He started at the bottom and began climbing straight up. Halfway up the hill, Andre was tired and couldn't go any farther. He heard Uncle Arthur laughing. "Follow the cowpath," shouted Uncle Arthur. Andre saw that the cows had worn a zig-zag path up the hillside. He took the cowpath the rest of the way. It was a longer distance than climbing straight up. But it turned out to be much easier.

1. Compare Andre's climb straight up the hill to the experiment you did in the investigation. _____

_____

_____

2. How is the cowpath like something you did in the investigation?

_____

3. Compare the two methods of climbing. Which method uses less force?

_____

4. Which method of climbing the hill uses the most distance?

_____

5. Which method of climbing the hill uses more work? _____

_____

Harcourt

Name _____

Date _____

Use Context to Determine/Confirm Word Meaning

Each of the underlined words has more than one meaning. Write the definition for each word, based on how it is used in the sentence.

1. Bobby set a school <u>record</u> for highest score in a basketball game.
record: _____

Janet had to <u>record</u> her day's activity in her diary.
record: _____

2. You can use a <u>spring</u> scale to measure force.
spring: _____

Many new plants grow in the <u>spring</u>.
spring: _____

3. A doorstop is a kind of <u>wedge</u> that has two inclined planes stuck back-to-back.
wedge: _____

Marie politely asked for another <u>wedge</u> of cake.
wedge: _____

4. Joseph used a <u>screw</u> to hold together his wagon.
screw: _____

After Jim was finished with the jar, his mother asked him to <u>screw</u> the lid back on.
screw: _____

Harcourt

Use with page F79.

Name _____

Date _____

What are Simple Machines?

Lesson Concept

Simple machines do not change the amount of work, but they reduce the amount of force needed to do the work, or they change the direction of the force.

Vocabulary

simple machine (F78)   **lever** (F78)   **inclined plane** (F79)

Underline the correct answer.

1. A _____ is an example of an inclined plane.

   A pulley   **B** rod   **C** lever   **D** board

2. When you pull something up an inclined plane you use less _____ than you use to pick it straight up.

   A energy   **B** force   **C** distance   **D** strength

3. Suppose you use a pulley attached to a pole to pull up a flag. What does the pulley do to the direction of the force?

   A changes the direction   **B** keeps the direction the same   **C** makes no change in the direction

4. Which of the following activities is NOT being done with a simple machine?

   A turning a doorknob to open a door   **B** prying open a paint can   **C** cutting out a picture from a magazine

5. A pair of scissors is a compound machine, because _____.

   A it is made of several simple machines   **B** it has a lever   **C** one blade is a wedge

Harcourt

Use with page F81.

Name _____

Date _____

Recognize Vocabulary

In the space provided, write the term in Column B that best fits the definition in Column A. Use each term only once.

Column A

1. _____
   a push or a pull

2. _____
   a change in position

3. _____
   the measure of how fast something moves over a certain distance

4. _____
   the force that pulls objects toward each other

5. _____
   a measure of the pull of gravity on an object

6. _____
   the measure of force it takes to move an object a certain distance

7. _____
   a tool that makes work easier

8. _____
   a flat surface set at an angle to another surface

9. _____
   a bar that moves on or around a fixed point

Column B

A motion

B work

C simple machine

D force

E gravity

F inclined plane

G lever

H speed

I weight

Harcourt

Use with pages **F64–F81.**

Name _____

Date _____

Write a Poem About a Machine

Expressive Writing–Poem

Write a poem about riding a bicycle or a theme park ride. In your poem, tell about the simple machines that make up the bicycle or the theme park ride. Include sensory words to describe the feeling of riding. Use the word web below to help you plan your poem.

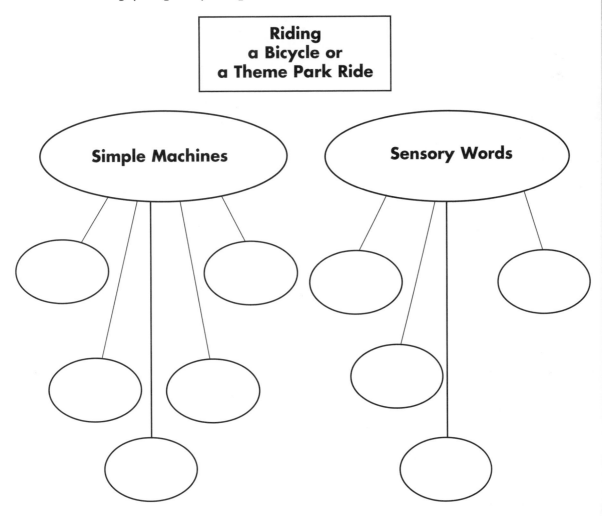

Riding a Bicycle or a Theme Park Ride

Simple Machines

Sensory Words

Harcourt

Unit Experiments
Grade 3

Harcourt

Name _____

Date _____

 **Experiment Log**

Use these pages to plan and conduct a science experiment to answer a question you may have.

1 Observe and Ask Questions

Make a list of questions you have about a topic. Then circle a question you want to investigate.

_____

_____

2 Form a Hypothesis

Write a hypothesis. A hypothesis is a suggested answer to the question you are investigating. You must be able to test the hypothesis.

_____

_____

3 Plan an Experiment

Identify and Control Variables

To plan your experiment, you must first identify the important variables. Complete the statements below.

The variable I will change is _____

_____

_____

The variable I will observe or measure is _____

_____

_____

The variables I will keep the same, or control, are _____

_____

_____

Name _____

 **Experiment Log**

Develop a Procedure and Gather Materials Write the steps you will follow to set up an experiment and collect data.

_____

_____

_____

_____

_____

_____

_____

_____

_____

_____

Materials List Look carefully at all the steps of your procedure and list all the materials you will use. Be sure your teacher approves your plan and your materials list before you begin.

_____

_____

_____

_____

_____

_____

_____

_____

Name _____

Experiment Log

4 Conduct the Experiment

Gather and Record Data | Follow your plan and collect data. Make a table or chart to record your data. Observe carefully. Record your observations and be sure to note anything unusual or unexpected. Use the space below and additional paper, if necessary.

Interpret Data | Make a graph of the data you have collected. Plot the data on a sheet of graph paper or use a software program.

5 Draw Conclusions and Communicate Results

Compare the hypothesis with the data and the graph. Then answer these questions.

Do the results of the experiment make you think that the hypothesis is true?

Explain. _____

_____

How would you revise the hypothesis? Explain. _____

_____

_____

What else did you observe during the experiment? _____

_____

_____

Prepare a presentation for your classmates to communicate what you have learned. Display your data table and graph.

Harcourt

Plant Growth and Water Sources

1 Observe and Ask Questions

Do different liquids affect how a plant grows? For example, will plants watered with tap water grow taller than plants watered with tap water mixed with vegetable oil, tap water mixed with dishwashing detergent, or tap water mixed with vinegar? Make a list of questions you have about plant growth and different liquids. Then circle the question you want to investigate.

_____

_____

_____

2 Form a Hypothesis

Write a hypothesis. A hypothesis is a suggested answer to the question you are investigating. You must be able to test the hypothesis.

_____

_____

_____

3 Plan an Experiment

To plan your experiment, you must first identify the important variables. Complete the statements below.

Identify and Control Variables

The variable I will change is_____

The variable I will observe or measure is _____

Harcourt

The variables I will keep the same, or *control*, are _____

_____

Develop a Procedure and Gather Materials

Write the steps you will follow to set up an experiment and collect data.

_____

_____

_____

_____

_____

_____

_____

_____

_____

_____

_____

_____

_____

Use extra sheets of blank paper if you need to write down more steps.

Materials List
Look carefully at all the steps of your procedure, and list all the materials you will use. Be sure that your teacher approves your plan and your materials list before you begin. _____

_____

_____

Harcourt

4 Conduct the Experiment

Gather and Record Data | Follow your plan and collect data. Use the chart below or a chart you design to record your data. **Observe** carefully. **Record** your observations, and be sure to note anything unusual or unexpected.

Plant Observations

	Height (mm)						
	Day 1	Day 2	Day 3	Day 4	Day 5	Day 6	Day 7

	Height (mm)						
	Day 8	Day 9	Day 10	Day 11	Day 12	Day 13	Day 14

Harcourt

Experiment Log

Observe

Interpret Data

Make a graph of the data you have collected. Plot the data on a sheet of graph paper or use a software program.

5 Draw Conclusions and Communicate Results

Compare the **hypothesis** with the data and graph, and then answer these questions.

1. Based on the results of the experiment, do you think the hypothesis is

true? Explain. _____

_____

_____

2. How would you revise the hypothesis? Explain. _____

_____

_____

3. What else did you observe during the experiment? _____

_____

_____

Prepare a presentation for your classmates to **communicate** what you have learned. Display your data table and graph.

Investigate Further Write another hypothesis that you might investigate.

_____

_____

_____

_____

Harcourt

Acid Rain and Plants

1 Observe and Ask Questions

How does acid rain affect plants? For example, does a plant that is exposed to acid rain change in any way? Make a list of questions you have about acid rain and plants. Then circle a question you want to investigate.

_____

_____

2 Form a Hypothesis

Write a hypothesis. A hypothesis is a suggested answer to the question you are investigating. You must be able to test the hypothesis.

_____

_____

3 Plan an Experiment

To plan your experiment, you must first identify the important variables. Complete the statements below.

Identify and Control Variables

The variable I will change is _____

_____

The variable I will observe or measure is _____

_____

The variables I will keep the same, or *control*, are _____

_____

Harcourt

Name _____

Experiment Log

Develop a Procedure and Gather Materials

Write the steps you will follow to set up an experiment and collect data.

_____

_____

_____

_____

_____

_____

_____

_____

_____

_____

_____

_____

_____

_____

Use extra sheets of blank paper if you need to write down more steps.

Materials List   Look carefully at all the steps of your procedure, and list all the materials you will use. Be sure that your teacher approves your plan and your materials list before you begin.

_____

_____

_____

_____

_____

Harcourt

4 Conduct the Experiment

Gather and Record Data Follow your plan and collect data. Use the chart below or a chart you design to record your data. **Observe** carefully. **Record** your observations, and be sure to note anything unusual or unexpected.

Observation Log

Plant Label	How the Plant Looks						
	Day 1	Day 2	Day 3	Day 4	Day 5	Day 6	Day 7

Plant Label	How the Plant Looks						
	Day 8	Day 9	Day 10	Day 11	Day 12	Day 13	Day 14

_____

_____

_____

Harcourt

Observe

Interpret Data | Make a two-column chart. Label the columns *Plant* and *Change*. List the plant labels in the first column. Compare your observations from Day 1 and Day 14. Summarize your findings in the second column.

5   Draw Conclusions and Communicate Results

Compare the **hypothesis** with the data and chart, and then answer these questions.

1. Based on the results of the experiment, do you think the hypothesis is

    true? Explain. _____

    _____

    _____

2. How would you revise the hypothesis? Explain. _____

    _____

    _____

    _____

3. What else did you **observe** during the experiment? _____

    _____

    _____

    _____

Prepare a presentation for your classmates to **communicate** what you have learned. Display your data table and chart.

Investigate Further | Write another hypothesis that you might investigate.

_____

_____

_____

Harcourt

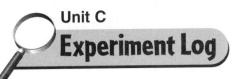
Decomposition of Trash in Landfills

1 Observe and Ask Questions

Substances that we do not or cannot recycle often end up in landfills. Landfills are places in which trash is buried. Some trash in landfills decays, or decomposes. Some trash does not decompose. Make a list of questions you have about trash that is buried in landfills. Then circle a question you want to investigate.

_____

_____

_____

_____

2 Form a Hypothesis

Write a hypothesis. A hypothesis is a suggested answer to the question you are investigating. You must be able to test the hypothesis.

_____

_____

3 Plan an Experiment

To plan your experiment, you must first identify the important variables. Complete the statements below.

Identify and Control Variables

The variable I will change is_____

The variable I will observe or measure is _____

_____

Harcourt

Name _____

The variables I will keep the same, or *control*, are _____

_____

_____

Develop a Procedure and Gather Materials

Write the steps you will follow to set up an experiment and collect data.

_____

_____

_____

_____

_____

_____

_____

_____

_____

_____

_____

_____

Use extra sheets of blank paper if you need to write down more steps.

Harcourt

Name _____

Materials List Look carefully at all the steps of your procedure, and list all the materials you will use. Be sure that your teacher approves your plan and your materials list before you begin. _____

_____

_____

4 Conduct the Experiment

Gather and Record Data Follow your plan and make careful observations. **Record** your **observations,** and be sure to note anything unusual or unexpected.

Observation of Decomposition

Type of Trash	Week 1	Week 2	Week 3	Week 4

Harcourt

Name _____

5 Draw Conclusions and Communicate Results

Compare the **hypothesis** with your observations, and then answer these questions.

1. Based on the results of the experiment, do you think the hypothesis is

true? Explain. _____

_____

2. How would you revise the hypothesis? Explain. _____

_____

3. What else did you **observe** during the experiment? _____

_____

_____

Investigate Further Write another hypothesis that you might investigate.

_____

_____

_____

Harcourt

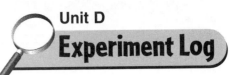
Air Pressure and Temperature

1 Observe and Ask Questions

Because air has weight, it presses on things. This is called air pressure.
Sometimes air presses harder against things than it does at other times.
Changes in air pressure are related to changes in air temperature. Make a list
of questions you have about the relationship between air pressure and air
temperature. Then circle a question you want to investigate.

_____

_____

_____

_____

_____

2 Form a Hypothesis

Write a hypothesis. A hypothesis is a suggested answer to the question you
are investigating. You must be able to test the hypothesis.

_____

_____

_____

3 Plan an Experiment

To plan your experiment, you must first identify the important variables.
Complete the statements on page WB322.

Harcourt

Name _____

Experiment Log

| Identify and Control Variables |

The variable I will change is _____

The variable I will observe or measure is _____

_____

The variables I will keep the same, or *control*, are the _____

_____

| Develop a Procedure and Gather Materials |

Write the steps you will follow to set up an experiment and collect data.

_____

_____

_____

_____

_____

CAUTION: Be careful when filling the bottle with hot tap water.

Use extra sheets of blank paper if you need to write down more steps.

| Materials List | Look carefully at all the steps of your procedure, and list all the materials you will use. Be sure that your teacher approves your plan and your materials list before you begin. _____

_____

_____

_____

_____

Name _____

4 Conduct the Experiment

| Gather and Record Data | Follow your plan. Make and **record** careful **observations. Draw** a picture of each can after the experiment is completed.

Bottle with Cold Tap Water

Bottle with Hot Tap Water

Observations _____

_____

_____

_____

_____

Harcourt

5 Draw Conclusions and Communicate Results

Compare the **hypothesis** with your observations, and then answer these questions.

1. Given the results of the experiment, do you think the hypothesis is true? Explain. _____

_____

_____

_____

2. How would you revise the hypothesis? Explain. _____

_____

_____

_____

_____

3. What else did you **observe** during the experiment? _____

_____

_____

Prepare a presentation that includes your drawings of the two bottles. **Communicate** what you have learned in this experiment.

| Investigate Further | Explain how you might use your results to make an instrument to measure changes in air pressure.

_____

_____

_____

_____

_____

Harcourt

Name _____

Date _____

The Freezing Point of Water

1 Observe and Ask Questions

What substances change the freezing point of water? Will mixing substances such as salt, sugar, or baking soda in ice water raise or lower its temperature? Make a list of questions you have about water's freezing point and how different substances affect it. Then circle a question you want to investigate.

_____

_____

_____

_____

_____

2 Form a Hypothesis

Write a hypothesis. A hypothesis is a suggested answer to the question you are investigating. You must be able to test the hypothesis.

_____

_____

3 Plan an Experiment

To plan your experiment, you must first identify the important variables. Complete the statements below.

Identify and Control Variables

The one variable I will change is _____

_____

The variable I will observe or measure is _____

_____

Harcourt

Name _____

The variables I will keep the same, or *control*, are _____

_____

_____

| Develop a Procedure and Gather Materials |

Write the steps you will follow to set up an experiment and collect data.

_____

_____

_____

_____

_____

_____

_____

_____

_____

_____

_____

_____

_____

_____

_____

_____

Use extra sheets of blank paper if you need to write down more steps.

Harcourt

Name _____

| Materials List | Look carefully at all the steps of your procedure and list all the materials you will use. Be sure that your teacher approves your plan and your materials list before you begin.

_____

_____

_____

_____

4   Conduct the Experiment

| Gather and Record Data | Follow your plan and collect data. Use the chart below or a chart you design to record your data. **Observe** carefully. **Record** your observations and be sure to note anything unusual or unexpected.

Observations: Freezing Point of Water with Added Substances

Substance	Temperature after 1 min in °C

Harcourt

Name _____

Experiment Log

| Interpret Data |

Make a graph of the data you have collected. Plot the graph on a sheet of graph paper or use a computer graphing program.

5 Draw Conclusions and Communicate Results

Compare your **hypothesis** with the data and graph, then answer these questions.

1. Based on the results of the experiment, do you think the hypothesis is

true? Why or why not? _____

_____

2. How would you revise the hypothesis? Be specific.

_____

_____

3. What else did you **observe** during the experiment?

_____

_____

Prepare a presentation for your classmates in order to **communicate** what you have learned. Display your data table and graph.

| Investigate Further | Write another hypothesis about water and how it freezes that you might investigate.

_____

_____

_____

_____

_____

_____

Harcourt

Solar Heat

1 Observe and Ask Questions

What does color have to do with the temperature of objects that are placed in sunlight? For example, which colors absorb the most heat from the sun? Make a list of questions you have about solar energy. Then circle a question you want to investigate.

_____

_____

_____

_____

2 Form a Hypothesis

Write a hypothesis. A hypothesis is a suggested answer to the question you are investigating. You must be able to test the hypothesis.

_____

_____

3 Plan an Experiment

To plan your experiment, you must first identify the important variables. Complete the statements below.

Identify and Control Variables

The variable I will change is _____

_____

The variable I will observe or measure is _____

_____

The variables I will keep the same, or *control*, are _____

_____

_____

Harcourt

Name _____

Experiment Log

| Develop a Procedure and Gather Materials |

Write the steps you will follow to set up an experiment and collect data.

_____

_____

_____

_____

_____

_____

_____

_____

_____

_____

_____

_____

_____

_____

_____

_____

Use extra sheets of blank paper if you need to write down more steps.

| Materials List | Look carefully at all the steps of your procedure, and list all the materials you will use. Be sure that your teacher approves your plan and your materials list before you begin.

_____

_____

_____

_____

Name _____

4 Conduct the Experiment

Gather and Record Data   Follow your plan and collect data. Use the table below or a table you design to record your data. **Observe** carefully. **Record** your observations, and be sure to note anything unusual or unexpected.

Color and Temperature Observations

Can Color	Temperature (taken every 30 minutes)					
	Measurement Times					
	30 min	1 hour	1 hour 30 min	2 hours	2 hours 30 min	3 hours

Other Observations

_____

_____

_____

_____

_____

_____

_____

Harcourt

Name _____

Experiment Log

Interpret Data

Make a graph of the data you have collected. Plot the graph on a sheet of graph paper, or use a software program.

5 Draw Conclusions and Communicate Results

Compare the **hypothesis** with the data and graph, and then answer these questions.

1. Based on the results of the experiment, do you think the hypothesis is true? Why or why not? Explain. _____

_____

_____

_____

2. How would you revise the hypothesis? Explain. _____

_____

_____

_____

3. What else did you **observe** during the experiment? _____

_____

_____

_____

Prepare a presentation for your classmates to **communicate** what you have learned. Display your data table and graph.

Investigate Further Write another hypothesis about solar heat that you might investigate.

_____

_____

_____

Harcourt